# INSTANT INFLUENCE & CHARISMA

•

## PAUL MCKENNA PH.D.

### EDITED BY HUGH WILLBOURN PH.D.

## BANTAM PRESS

LONDON · TORONTO · SYDNEY · AUCKLAND · JOHANNESBURG

TRANSWORLD PUBLISHERS
61–63 Uxbridge Road, London W5 5SA
www.transworldbooks.co.uk

Transworld is part of the Penguin Random House group of companies
whose addresses can be found at global.penguinrandomhouse.com

First published in Great Britain in 2015 by Bantam Press
an imprint of Transworld Publishers

A CIP catalogue record for this book
is available from the British Library.

ISBN 9780593075661

Typeset in 11/17pt Palatino by Julia Lloyd Design
Printed and bound by Clays Ltd, Bungay, Suffolk

Penguin Random House is committed to a sustainable
future for our business, our readers and our planet. This book
is made from Forest Stewardship Council® certified paper.

1 3 5 7 9 10 8 6 4 2

*Also by Paul McKenna*

THE 3 THINGS THAT WILL CHANGE YOUR DESTINY TODAY!

FREEDOM FROM EMOTIONAL EATING

THE HYPNOTIC GASTRIC BAND

I CAN MAKE YOU SMARTER

I CAN MAKE YOU HAPPY

I CAN MAKE YOU THIN

I CAN MAKE YOU THIN: 90-DAY SUCCESS JOURNAL

I CAN MAKE YOU THIN: LOVE FOOD, LOSE WEIGHT! (illustrated)

CONTROL STRESS

I CAN MAKE YOU SLEEP

I CAN MAKE YOU RICH

QUIT SMOKING TODAY

INSTANT CONFIDENCE

CHANGE YOUR LIFE IN 7 DAYS

I CAN MEND YOUR BROKEN HEART (with Hugh Willbourn)

THE HYPNOTIC WORLD OF PAUL McKENNA

www.**transworldbooks**.co.uk

# CONTENTS

**Thanks to:**

Dr Richard Bandler, Dr Robert Cialdini, Dr Ronald Ruden, Dr Graham Wagstaff, Simon Cowell, Mike Osborne, Kate Davey, Michael Neill, Michael Breen, John Arroyo, Steve King, Doug Young, Janine Giovanni, Larry Finlay, Robert Kirby, Paul Rice, Adrian Pearmund, Mari Roberts, Neil Reading and Matthew Christian.

To all the people who participated in the experiments that led to the development of this system.

Finally, Dr Hugh Willbourn, whose work ethic and deeply rich understanding of people never ceases to amaze me.

**CODE: TC15U507N**

Go to **www.paulmckenna.com/downloads** and type in this
code to access your complimentary hypnosis programme.

# READ THIS FIRST

The book comes with a card inside the cover. The card has your unique code to download an audio track and a video track from www.paulmckenna.com/downloads.

If the card is missing or lost, please refer to the instructions on the opposite page.

The video contains footage demonstrating psycho-sensory techniques which form a vital part of this program. **You must** use each of these techniques as directed to increase your influence and release your inner charisma.

The audio track contains a hypnotic trance. You should listen to it as directed, only in a quiet place where you expect to be undisturbed for twenty minutes. Do not listen to it while driving a vehicle or operating any kind of machinery.

Every element of this system is vital. Read the book, watch the video and listen to the audio exactly as directed.

When you read the book, you absorb the information at the level of conscious understanding. The trance on the audio track addresses your unconscious mind directly, and the video will show you the precise movements entailed in the techniques it illustrates.

The system requires all three of these elements, so please use all of them.

# 1
.
# WHAT YOU NEED TO KNOW

## What you need to know

Welcome to an easier life! Welcome to a world where people are more friendly, doors are opened, opportunities are offered and help is easier to find. Welcome to a world where people cooperate, work flows more easily, meetings are not boring and life is more fulfilling.

Why are some people so good at getting their own way? How do they sail through life so easily? They are not super-beautiful, super-talented or super-intelligent and yet people are willing to help them wherever they go. How do they do it? These people apply the universal principles of influence with everyone they meet. Some of them have learned from their upbringing or education. Others have studied hard, and for some it seems it just comes naturally. When you have used this system you will learn how to be just like them.

The system creates social confidence. It shows you how to make an impact and how to protect yourself from unwanted influences, how to be a more eloquent communicator and understand how the modern world works. I firmly believe this system should be taught in every school.

## The difference

The difference between winners and losers is that winners are the sort of people who read this book from end to end, who will watch the video and use the hypnotic trance and practise the exercises. Losers will quit halfway through or read about the techniques but not do the practice. Losers quit after one attempt – whether it works or not. Winners keep working and practising until they have overwhelming evidence of success.

Increasing your influence and charisma will have an enormous effect on the rest of your life. Imagine that for the rest of your life you were 10 per cent more influential. Think of all the extra opportunities you would gain. Now imagine if you were 20 per cent more influential, or 30 per cent more influential. What about 40 per cent or even more? I very strongly recommend that you dedicate yourself for the few hours necessary to mastering the techniques in this book to improve your career, your marriage and your happiness.

Do you have a difficult boss? Troublesome employees? Family conflicts? Do you avoid public gatherings? If there is any part of your life where you could use some extra influence and charisma, read on. Whatever your current situation you will learn how to massively improve it.

## At last we understand what charisma really is

People used to think that some people were lucky and others weren't. Scientists have now proved that is not true. There are specific, learnable patterns of behaviour that will change your luck. People think charisma is magical and elusive and unattainable. It certainly looks like magic, but after twenty years of study and ten years of living in Los Angeles among some of the most charismatic people in the world, I have cracked the code. We now have the secret of charisma. There is a step-by-step process that you can take through this book that cannot fail to make you more charismatic. Will it make you George Clooney? I don't know, but your ability to be charismatic and magnetically interesting to others will be massively enhanced.

Charisma is now attainable. We can understand all its constituent parts and we have the psychological technology to build it in you.

Charisma is a glowing human energy. We all have charisma, but for many people it has been stifled or hidden. Too many people have been told they are not good enough so they have not developed the skills of making friends, making people happy, telling engaging stories and touching people emotionally. But we can learn all of these skills and more, and as you do so you will find they are all much, much easier than you might think.

You will capture people's attention and hold it. They will think there is something beguiling and intriguing about you. At first glance charisma seems to be all about you. But charisma is all about the effect you have on others. When you are charismatic, you make everyone you talk to feel like they are the most important person in the room.

When we hear about famously charismatic people like the

Dalai Lama, Martin Luther King, Sophia Loren, Mick Jagger or Bill Clinton, over and over again we hear people say things like, 'He was genuinely interested,' 'She was so warm' or 'He made me feel great'.

Charisma is not always big, bright or brash. Some charismatic people have a relatively low profile. They are charming and friendly and approachable and good company. They make all the friends they need, they get invited to the right parties and they make the right contacts. When they make suggestions people tend to agree with them. They inspire loyalty and trust. When they form a team, that team is successful even if it doesn't make a big fuss or a lot of noise. This is quiet charisma and it is just as valuable and powerful as the louder, shinier varieties. Some of you will be suited to a high-profile, some to a low-profile, and some will easily manage both. At this stage we don't know how you will be charismatic, so keep an open mind as you work through this system and find which styles suit you best.

Your charisma will make a difference at home and at work. Charisma is the key to turning around a difficult situation, to rescuing a business, to making a performance amazing, to healing a family, to launching your career and to leading a team to victory.

Your charisma will inspire people to bravery, to achievement and to success. It allows you to become the best possible you: charming to be around, trustworthy and authentic. This is your power to be treasured and valued.

## What you can achieve

When you have integrated the learning in this system, your ability to influence will be available instantly and automatically and you will have released the essence of your own, personal charisma. These achievements are neither simple nor small. I can guarantee that when you use all the techniques in the system you will instantly increase your power to influence, but there will be even more to learn and to achieve as you gain more experience of using these techniques. The more you practise and the more you use this system, the greater the benefits. I will show you how to release and nurture your own charisma, but it will be your application, focus and practice that will make it truly flourish. You will find it easier to get people to like and trust you, and to say yes to you.

As you become charismatic and influential, you will be acquiring many other qualities. You will increase your likeability, confidence, flexibility, self-knowledge, authenticity and persistence. You will enhance your sociability, your listening skills, your objectivity, your independence and your knowledge of social psychology. You will learn to fill a room with energy. You will increase your power yet also your prudence. If that list looks a little overwhelming, don't worry. All of this will be done in straightforward, easy stages. My job is to help you change, not to stuff you full of information. Your unconscious mind will take what is best for you and integrate it so that when you have completed using this whole system, you will have massively magnified your charisma and ability to influence. Everything you learn here has a purpose. This book is not written to satisfy your curiosity. This is a manual for personal change. Use it and change.

## The difference that makes a difference

What is the difference between being the average man or woman in the street and being in the top 10 per cent of successful and powerful people? Is it talent? Is it hard work? Is it about having the right parents? Over the last twenty-five years I've met a good many of the successful, rich and powerful people all over the Western world and I would say that all three of those factors have a part to play. But it is also possible to be successful and powerful without talent, without hard work and without knowing even who your parents are. More than any of those factors, what matters most is being able to influence your fellow human beings.

Some of the most successful and charismatic people I know are not particularly good-looking. They were born in poverty. Some suffered an abusive childhood. But they are not victims. They connected to their inner charisma and that alone was enough to change their destiny.

Real influence is not assertiveness. Someone can do a dozen assertiveness training courses and still be seen as authoritarian or pushy or dictatorial. Charisma is different. Charisma allows you to motivate people to do jobs that are hard, difficult and demanding and yet focus on the achievement, teamwork and benefits. Charisma produces an energy that is uplifting. It is not about driving people to exhaustion, or forcing customers to sign up. You don't have to hunt people down. Charisma attracts people to work hard for you and your customers to buy your services.

Charisma is a way to work smart, not hard.

Charismatic people are not driven. They are inspired. I have one good friend who is a super successful international producer and star. He is rarely in the office at 8 a.m. He can work an eighteen-hour day if necessary, but most often he gets up at midday, and each day aims to make one good decision.

## Get out of the way

Have you ever watched yourself on video? Did you see things about yourself that you didn't notice at the time? I remember watching a video of myself giving an impromptu talk and I was embarrassed at how many times I umm-ed and ahh-ed. I had not been aware of doing so during the talk, but I made a decision to stop doing it. At first I had to be very conscious and careful, but very soon I had changed my habit and my speech pattern was changed.

Much of the time we are not aware of the things we

have been doing that work against our primary intention. I commonly meet people who are speak too fast or too much or repeat themselves. They don't notice it. They just have a vague feeling of anxiety and a compulsion to convey their meaning as quickly as possible. Overwhelmed by their own anxiety, they fail to pick up the signals from the people to whom they are talking, and they undermine their own communication. Very often people like this just need to trust themselves and get out of their own way. On the path to charisma and influence we all need to get to know ourselves a little better.

## Invisible influence

When I told a friend I was writing this book, he was very sceptical. I asked him why.

'Well,' he replied, 'people are perfectly nice and helpful and friendly. Why would you need to go around influencing them?'

He believed that he 'just asked' for things, and he got them. In a sense, he was right. However, his 'just asking' is always perfectly phrased and perfectly timed. He is a natural influencer, but he was completely unaware of his formidable talent. He knows just what to say and when to say it. Wherever he goes he makes friends and he always seems to meet the right person at the right time. People like him and the way he expresses himself. He doesn't believe he is doing anything special, like 'influencing people'. He is just being himself, and that of course makes him even more influential.

Of course he is unique, as you are. But the skills and techniques he uses naturally can be learned by all of us, and I have put them all, and more, in this book.

You will learn a great deal from this system, and the more you use it and the more you practise the more influential you will become. However, I believe my job will really be done when you are no longer thinking about everything you have learned here. You just find that people are perfectly nice and helpful and friendly and when you ask for things you tend to get them. That is when you are truly influential.

Influence is often most effective when it is not visible to the person influenced. Many years ago I heard Allen Carr interviewed on the radio. Allen was completely addicted to cigarettes and visited a hypnotherapist to help him to quit. A few minutes after he came out of the session he lit a cigarette. Then, as he told the interviewer, a few days later he thought to himself, 'I don't need these. Each cigarette is just creating the stress that I am calming with the next one. I can just stop!' And with that thought he threw away his cigarettes.

The way Allen told the story, the hypnotherapist had totally failed and he, Allen, had an insight a few days later that changed his life and he became a crusader to stop other people smoking.

As I heard him tell the story I thought, 'Wow! What a brilliant hypnotherapist!' He not only got Allen to quit, he made him think it was his own idea, and that made it even more powerful. Allen would never be able to say, 'Well it worked for a while then the hypnosis wore off.' It had become his own idea and his own achievement. And even more wonderful, the compulsion to stop smoking in Allen was so huge that he not only stopped himself but he created an international business helping people to quit. In my opinion, Allen met a first-class hypnotherapist who was all the more successful precisely because his influence was invisible.

## Unconscious competence

When we do things very, very well, we often don't notice. My friend Ryan Seacrest is widely considered one of the most successful broadcasters and producers in the world. I watched when he stood in for Larry King on his worldwide chat show, and I told him, 'You are such a good interviewer.'

'Really?' he said. 'I just talk to the guys. I'm interested in them.'

Ryan is right. He just talks to his interviewees. It looks and sounds easy because it is natural. The conversation flows and people open up to him because he really is warm and he really is interested. He is fascinated by people and he is curious and he really, really wants to know. So Ryan doesn't need a script or a clipboard of prompt questions. His genuine enthusiasm does the job for him. He is charismatic because he is not trying.

## Manipulation

When I mentioned this book to another friend he thought it was a bad idea. He immediately imagined I would make people scheming and manipulative and unpleasant, and thousands of readers would be unleashed to indulge themselves at everyone else's expense. He had a very negative view of what it would be like to be influential and charismatic. He imagined becoming arrogant, uncaring and self-indulgent; neither needing nor wishing to pay attention to the feelings of others.

That's not the plan. In fact, my goal is the complete opposite. In my experience most people want to behave decently.

I have met some people who have behaved very badly and in every case I believe they have acted from a position of fear or inadequacy. They have tried to use others – and on some occasions tried to take advantage of me – to make up for the lack they feel in themselves. However, I believe that deep down, almost everyone wishes to be liked and to be kind. Very, very few people are deliberately malevolent. Almost all evil acts, whether small and petty or large and monstrous, are committed by people who failed to find a more humane and healthy means to meet their needs.

As a general rule, people behave badly when they are frightened or greedy (or both) and they can't think of a better option. This book is full of better options, so far from making people behave badly it will help us all to get more of what we want by being more resourceful and more truthful.

I strongly believe that in this busy and chaotic world, if you have a positive intention, it is a good thing to be influential. Furthermore, the most powerful form of influence comes from being true to yourself and your deepest values, and I believe that when we are freed from fear and greed we will come from a place of integrity. This system will help you be the very best version of yourself so you can present yourself, your ideas or your products in the best possible light. That truly will make the world a better place.

## Powerful requests

Some people think manipulation is always a bad thing. It has been given a bad reputation by liars, conmen and high-pressure salesmen. However, if you have a legitimate request, it is both sensible and reasonable to make it as powerful as possible.

If you think about it, you are constantly asking people to change their behaviour for your benefit. The simplest request 'please pass me the butter' is a method of changing someone's behaviour, and there is nothing wrong with it. Unfortunately, there are times when people sometimes need a bit of persuasion to do the right thing.

Large corporations have customer service and sales staff who are trained to follow scripts. These scripts are ways of controlling conversations so that customers follow a path that allows the corporation to sell its products or to service the needs of its customers in a way that is most efficient for the corporation. We are manipulated by those scripts.

But there are times when those scripts are inadequate and do not address issues that arise in the real world. That is when I find it useful to make my requests more persuasive. I don't see that as a bad thing. I do see it as presenting the facts in such a way that the other party feels themselves compelled to act in a manner that meets my needs.

## Defence

Of course, there will always be people who try to manipulate or trick other people for their own selfish purposes. The best defence against manipulation is to see the tricks that are being used. This book will help you defend yourself. You will see through their tricks and you will not be caught by them.

I believe also that you will have more courage and more skills to stand back from some of the vast autonomous influences that dominate public discourse and you will be willing and able to stand up for your own personal beliefs. Over time, that will make you a more powerful and influential person and the whole world a better place.

Ultimately most influential people are true to themselves. The foundation for the richest, most compelling forms of influence is the integrity of being true to yourself.

## Freedom

Ultimately, as you master the skills and concepts in this book, you will gain a freedom that few others have. As you become aware of the myriad influences that are installed within you and at work in the world all around, you gain the freedom to choose how much you let them guide your behaviour. Inevitably, you will become more self-sufficient and more confident. You will become more discerning.

Some of the influences around us are benign and others are exploitative. As you see them you can judge for yourself and decide which to accept and which to reject.

You will also find that you have a satisfying response to a great many everyday situations. Dealing with buying and selling, with bureaucracies, with difficult neighbours and wayward family members will all become much, much easier.

When you feel good about yourself you make others feel good and the world is a better place, by just that little bit. This book will help you, and hundreds of thousands of kind and well-intentioned people like yourself, to wield your influence to positive effect. You will find cooperative ways to achieve your goals and desires, to spread positive attitudes and to bring about healthy solutions to conflicts.

I have explained the principles that underlie the techniques in this book because as you understand them you will know better how to use them. However, much more important than that, you will soon be applying the principles in new ways to develop your own ways to influence people. You are not limited by the techniques here. The more you use them, and the more you understand the principles, the more easily you will develop your own versions and variations.

## By you or against you

We cannot choose whether or not to engage with powers of influence. They are already here and all around us. They are already working on you. You are continually on the receiving end of messages designed to sway your opinions and determine your behaviour. As you read on, you will discover many, many occasions when your decision was prompted by outside forces. However, by the time you have finished this book you will be free to choose how to respond. The only thing you can't do is choose not to be involved.

We live inside a field of countless influences. I believe that it is right that we all know more about influence so that we can move away from mass movements and mass marketing, and make our own decisions based on our values.

The world is full of businesses trying to persuade you that their goods and services will make you happy. Don't worry! Buy things! Be happy! Buying things does make you happy briefly, but in the long term happiness comes from living by your values and finding what you enjoy doing, rather than buying stuff or doing what other people have persuaded you to do. It may take a little longer to work out your own values and goals but the pay-off is vastly better.

## Fortune

When I started learning about hypnosis I was working for Colin Mason at Chiltern Radio. Colin had a military background and was a bit of a legend in radio. I was a maverick and, if the truth be told, was probably unbearably cocky. One day I got into an argument with Colin, telling him – the managing director with years of experience – how he should run his station.

He quite rightly asked, 'What do you know, at twenty-one years of age?'

I blurted out, 'I'm going to be a millionaire by the time I'm thirty.'

'OK,' he said, 'let's have a sportsman's bet. Write it down and sign it.'

A few years ago we met up and he showed me that piece of paper and kindly offered his congratulations. How did I do it? I believe that my fascination with hypnosis and influence played a huge part.

I was obsessed with hypnosis and spent all my free time learning and practising. While I was still working as a DJ I started doing my hypnotic shows. As my career as a hypnotist was taking off I was also getting more and more offers of work as a DJ. I moved to Capital Radio. When I was there I found more of my ideas were being taken up at radio production meetings. More girls would go out with me. I don't believe I suddenly became more handsome or a better DJ. I realized the difference must be that I had become more influential. The language of persuasion had become second nature to me. I was using it without noticing I was doing so.

Ambition, persistence, talent and hard work all have a part to play in building a career, but I believe the power to influence is crucial. Whether you are going for promotion or you need to get backing for an idea, you need to be able to influence the people around you.

I have spent the last thirty years developing this book through the trial-and-error process of building my own career. I have been fortunate. But I have also worked hard to develop my ideas and get them across to other people. Nowadays I get hired more often to talk about influence than any other subject. Influence is the key to success. Read on and join me on the road to good fortune.

## Why does this work so well?

This is a practical book. It is not an armchair read. It is not a thesis, or a dissertation on the theory of influence. It is a system that has to be applied. When you apply it, you will make more money. You will get dates more easily. You will give better, more impactful presentations. You will win more arguments and make more sales. Above all, you will be more free to express your own values and live a more personally rewarding life.

This system works because you don't just read about it or think about it, you use it. So right now I would like you to think of at least three situations where you want to increase your influence or charisma. Maybe you can think of more than three, maybe you can think of ten or twenty situations. Maybe you want to secure a promotion at work or sort out a problem in the family. You may wish to improve a relationship or enhance a romance. Maybe you are a performer and you want to enhance your act or maybe you are a manager and you want to inspire your team. Choose at least three situations that matter to you in which you want more influence and charisma and write them down, right now. Keep that piece of paper so that you have a record of it when you have achieved your goal.

And today, that is all you need to do. Just write them down. As soon as you have done that, your unconscious is aware of them as goals and will reference them as you read and work through the exercises in this book and on the audio and video tracks. I would like you to read the whole book, complete all the exercises and use all the audio video tracks before you deliberately tackle any of these situations.

## Audio

As soon as you have half an hour to spare when you can be undisturbed in a quiet place, listen to the trance on the audio download. Many people find that it is convenient to listen in bed before going to sleep. The trance is guided hypnosis that will empower the source of your charisma and begin to imprint the patterns of hypnotic language. There is no need to make an effort to listen because your unconscious mind is learning all the time and will start to absorb new techniques and information regardless of your conscious intention. Just relax, let the sounds wash over you and if it is appropriate you may fall asleep afterwards.

Very importantly, listen to the trance every day for a week, then use it again as often as you wish.

You may well find that you are more powerful and influential in many situations without any deliberate effort at all. However, to install and retain the full benefits of the system, please use all the elements exactly as directed. As you integrate the system it will become natural to you to be influential whenever you wish. It will be so natural, you may scarcely recognize how much better you handle things.

This whole package of book, audio and video is designed so that each section and chapter and exercise prepares you for the material that follows. As you follow it step by step, your comprehension and competence are reinforced, so that when you complete it you know what to do, you know how to do it and you know when to do it.

# IN A NUTSHELL

- You are already being influenced

- You must practise all the techniques and exercises as directed

- Everything in this book will either be used by you or against you

# NEXT STEPS

➤ Write down at least three situations in which you wish to become influential and charismatic

➤ Listen to the audio download trance at least seven times in the next week

➤ Listen to the audio download trance as often as you wish thereafter

# 2

·

# THE FOUNDATIONS
# OF INFLUENCE
# AND CHARISMA

## The foundations of influence and charisma

You are already influencing people. To become a master of influence you must start by understanding what you are already doing. We all influence each other all the time. We can't help it. Influence is part of our very existence. Every time you shake hands you are using influence, by triggering a pattern so deeply ingrained in our culture that holding out your hand influences the other person to do the same. When you ask a question, you are not forcing anyone to do anything, but you trigger a social pattern which creates a strong pressure on them to reply.

You can influence or be influenced in less than a second with a single look. Think of coming home from work. You walk in the door and your partner gives you a look. In that moment you know what sort of an evening you will have. With their look and the posture and tone of their whole body, he or she shows you their feelings, their mood and their degree of willingness to engage.

We even influence each other without any deliberate intention at all. Imagine you wake up tomorrow and you feel fabulous. You know you are going to have a great day. You are happy, your eyes sparkle and you smile a great deal. You meet someone who sees you smiling and they smile back. In that moment, your feeling has positively affected that person.

Smiles are easy to notice and easy to understand, but they are just the tip of the iceberg. We have an amazingly sophisticated sensitivity to each other's emotional states. Our emotions are much more subtle and sophisticated than our verbal language. Even if we can't formulate a precise verbal description, we still know exactly how we feel. And our feelings directly affect other people, regardless of what we are saying. Every one of us is constantly transmitting our feelings and moods to each other.

For example, imagine asking someone for some help. Regardless of what they say, if they are reluctant, you immediately know it. You feel it. You don't have to think about it or translate anything or interpret anything. We are continually transmitting information like that about our internal states.

Sometimes we try to hide our feelings. We may even be successful, at least with some people. However, we always transmit some information about how we are feeling. Generally speaking, you will fool people who are fooling themselves to the same extent as you, even if they are unaware of doing so. The more work a person has done to get to know themselves, the less easy they are to deceive.

There are times when we don't know what we feel. And sometimes we have one idea about how we feel and our body is signalling something else. Whatever we choose to do we are always transmitting something, even if that something is 'I'm hiding what I feel'.

By the same token, we never see a person without some sense of how they are feeling. Even if we get it wrong or we misunderstand them, we always understand them somehow: as friendly or threatening, as attractive, scary or interesting.

None of us have any choice about whether or not we transmit or receive influences. This is why your feelings are an enormously powerful source of influence on the people around you. The knack is to *control* the influence we have on other people. This system enables you to do that.

## Parents

Parents are probably the best hypnotists in the world. Children learn by imitation and up to the age of seven they are like sponges, absorbing understanding from everything and everyone around them. We all learn to speak by imitation. Children can learn several languages at once up to the age of about seven. Then when rational, methodical thinking takes over, learning actually slows down. It is far, far harder for an older child to learn a language than for a seven-year-old.

Our characters are also profoundly influenced by major moments of emotional intensity up to the age of about seven. If a child has an intense experience of disappointment and is blamed, they can absorb that into their idea of themselves so that they believe they are no good. By the same token, if when you are very young you have a stroke of good luck and you are told you are lucky, you integrate that into your understanding of yourself and the world. It becomes a filter so that you interpret more events as opportunities for good fortune. You become lucky.

Childhood experiences are the raw material for the software we use for the rest of our lives. Parents read us stories, cuddle us and give us rules to live by. But most of all they influence us through their behaviour. What they do is far, far more influential than what they say, because above all we learn by imitation. A simplistic version of development psychology can give the impression that parents are therefore to blame for all problems of their children. That's not true. No one can be the perfect parent. British psychoanalyst Donald Winnicott debunked that myth with his notion of the 'good-enough' parent. You can't be the perfect parent, but you can give a good example of being imperfect. Being loving, consistent and honest is definitely good enough.

We now know how these early influences are integrated, so we are able to rearrange them and neutralize negative messages. We can now install new positive self-beliefs and optimize the filters by which we understand the world. Whatever we inherited, we can now restructure so that we achieve the most from the opportunities we are offered by life.

## Feeling good, acting powerful

Let's start by ensuring that your own basic state is positive and powerful. We now know that our posture and body language affects other people. Social psychologist Amy Cuddy of the Harvard Business School has become famous for her work showing that our posture also influences ourselves.

Cuddy conducted an experiment which demonstrated that both physiology and behaviour are directly affected by posture. Cuddy's subjects were not given any guidance. They were simply asked to sit or stand in specific poses. Then they were put through a gruelling job interview. Their behaviour and performance were assessed by judges who had no information about what they had been asked to do. Subjects who had been given the power poses significantly outperformed those who had been given low-status poses.

Just two minutes in the poses was enough to make significant physiological and behavioural differences. The behaviour of the power-pose subjects was more confident and assertive, their levels of cortisol (the stress hormone) were lower and their levels of testosterone (the confidence hormone) were elevated.

Cuddy used three simple common poses. The wonderful thing about these poses is that even when we believe our thoughts are unstoppable or our feelings are overwhelming we can always simply move our limbs and take up these positions. Within two minutes of moving into these poses, our physiology and hence our whole state is changed.

I am optimistic but also sceptical so I tested the poses myself. I felt great, but I still wasn't sure. Maybe I had just used them to boost my natural optimism. So I turned to a close friend who had a tendency to be a bit diffident and self-effacing. The greeting on her voicemail sounded like she was apologizing for existing. I didn't explain anything. I just asked her to do the poses for two minutes each. Then I asked her to re-record her voicemail greeting. Boom! The difference was startling. Now she sounded like a chief executive.

I've shared Cuddy's amazing work with many, many friends and clients since. Some of them go to the bathroom to do the poses before important meetings, and they notice that even walking from the bathroom to the meeting room people treat them differently. They exude power, authority and confidence.

I believe Amy Cuddy's work is simple, brilliant and powerful, and I want you to try it right now. If you find these exercises uncomfortable or strange, or if you find yourself saying, 'This is weird' or 'This doesn't really suit me' or 'This isn't really right', then you *absolutely must* practise them until they feel as natural and comfortable as sitting in your favourite chair. If these postures feel silly or unusual or bad or difficult for you, that means that for years you have been training yourself to sit or stand in low-status poses. You have been telling people you are an underdog. Indirectly and unintentionally you have been inviting people to put themselves in power over you. Starting right now, you must do these poses until they feel completely natural and comfortable.

If you already find these poses natural and easy, or if they feel familiar, that is excellent, you already have an excellent base for influencing others, but you will still benefit from doing them as they will enhance your power and influence even more.

These poses are great preparation before a presentation, an interview or an important performance. If you need privacy, go and do them in the bathroom. Do not try to repeat them or hold them during an interview or meeting or performance. Do them beforehand.

## POWER POSES

POSE 1 'Wonder Woman':
hands on hips

POSE 2 'Winner':

arms up high like star

POSE 3 'Boss':

hands behind head, elbows wide

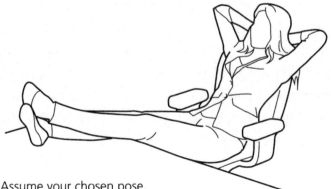

1. Assume your chosen pose.

2. Hold it for 2 minutes.

3. Relax and carry on with your life, energized and empowered.

## Golden thread

Sir Roger Moore told me that when he first went to acting school he had a teacher who asked him, 'How tall are you?'

'Six foot one,' he replied.

'So now stand as though you are six foot one,' said the teacher. Roger straightened up. And from that day onwards he started getting more work.

I have a simple exercise that creates this effect and I now use it as a follow up to the power poses. I imagine that there is a golden thread coming down from the sky, going through the very top of my head and down to my spine, which is holding me upright. I imagine this thread holding me upright and taking my weight so I am relaxed but with a tall, upright posture. You can't walk around all day in a Wonder Woman pose, but you can imagine a golden thread holding you upright. It takes just a couple of seconds to remember it, to let your body respond and to feel the benefits. It is particularly useful if you are tired or stressed or have spent too long hunched over a computer. Use it as often as you can, and after a while you will notice that your body wants to keep that relaxed, upright posture as often as it can.

## Internal dialogue

What do you do when you make a mistake? Do you say to yourself, 'Excellent, another learning experience'? Or do you say, 'Bloody idiot'? We all know that in the long-term we do learn from our mistakes but in the moment many people have a habit of self-criticism which, over time, can have a very corrosive effect.

You will know, if you have read my previous books, that we all have this inner voice which we use to think. We are so accustomed to using it we scarcely notice it. But take a moment now and pay attention to your inner voice. Think, for example, about choosing what you will eat for lunch: a salad? a sandwich? a burger? As you run through the alternatives in your mind you use that internal voice.

Now listen and pay attention to the tone of the voice. Is it relaxed and friendly? Or tense and stressed? Notice where you imagine the voice. Is it in the centre of your head or towards the back? Make a note of the location.

Almost all of us criticize ourselves in a critical tone of voice. At weight-loss seminars I meet many people who think they must give themselves a hard time in order to lose weight. Negative self-criticism not only doesn't work, it is actually bad for you. Research shows that weight gain is linked to stress. I used to have a very harsh, internal critical voice, but I have learned how to change that voice, and in the next exercise I would like to show you how to change your internal voice and, as a result, change how you feel.

## CHANGING THE INTERNAL VOICE

1.  Think about a time when you criticized yourself severely, and remember what you said.

2.  Listen carefully to your inner voice and notice where it is, what tone it has and how loud it is.

3.  Now change the tone of the voice so it sounds like Mickey Mouse or another crazy cartoon character.

4.  Next, hold your hand up in front of you with the thumb pointing upwards and imagine floating that voice away from your head and out to your thumb.

5.  Now, imagine hearing the same critical comment but with your voice coming from your thumb and speaking like Mickey Mouse.

6.  Now, listen again and hear everything that might be useful while feeling relaxed and amused by the silly tone of voice you are hearing.

I'd like you to practise this exercise so that every time you start to criticize yourself, you use this voice and move the voice to the end of your thumb. Sometimes you need to hear what that critical voice says. Keep the content the same for the moment, but when you move and change it like this, you change your response. Instead of feeling bad, you can feel good and still learn from any mistakes you may have made.

## Voice power

Now let's change the everyday voice you use for other types of thinking. Let's make it a warm, reassuring, confident voice. Think of a time when you felt very happy and full of confidence and energy and remember how your own voice sounded then. Or you can think of someone who is confident and upbeat and remember their voice.

Now, as you think, use this new, confident, happy voice. Say a few words to yourself using that really warm, reassuring voice and notice how you feel. You should already feel good, just from hearing that voice.

My good friend Michael Breen has created an ingenious way to make this positive voice even more influential in your everyday life, so I've laid it out in an exercise format here so you can find it, refer to it and practise it until it becomes second nature to you.

## CHANGING THE EXTERNAL VOICE

1.  Think of how your voice sounds when you are full of happiness, confidence and positive energy.

2.  Use that voice for your internal dialogue. Whatever you say to yourself, say it with this voice.

3.  Notice that you feel happier, more confident and energized.

4.  If you don't get an immediate effect, keep using it and adjusting the voice until you notice that your own feeling is positively affected.

5.  Now, listen even more carefully and, while you speak out loud, make your own voice sound more and more like your happy, confident, energized internal voice.

6.  The two voices don't have to sound immediately identical. Keep adjusting your speaking voice so that it takes on more and more of the characteristics of the happy, confident internal voice and you feel the same good feelings when you speak aloud as when you are thinking to yourself. You can continue to do this, little by little, over many occasions until you are completely accustomed to sounding and feeling happy and confident.

## The myth of having no influence

I have met some people who tell me they have no influence. No one pays them attention. When they stand at the bar, they are always the last to be served; when they talk, someone always cuts across them. They say they have no influence on other people at all. I tell them that, on the contrary, they have a massive influence. They are signalling to the rest of the world that everyone can ignore them as long as they want. Their problem is not that they have no influence, rather it is that they have an influence they don't want.

The renowned American therapist and author Jay Haley famously remarked, 'We cannot not influence each other.' When we realize the truth of Jay Haley's statement, the first step towards mastering our influence over other people is to take charge of the influences we are *already* creating.

## Overcoming sabotage

All sorts of people have come to see me because they have had serious problems with the people around them. Sometimes it has been in the personal areas of marriage and family, other times in business or show business. Most of them have said to me they feel powerless.

The complete opposite was true. The most common reason for their problems, regardless of the area, has been that their internal states have been transmitting very powerful influences with an effect directly opposed to what they want.

One woman was so anxious to be liked that everyone around her found her anxiety unbearable. The more anxious she was, the more they moved away and the more desperate she became. She pretended she didn't care, but her desperation was so intense that what people experienced was 'I'm desperate and I'm pretending I'm not'.

Using hypnosis I helped her to relax and then asked her to step into her own future and to experience how she would feel when she knew that she was truly liked, loved and appreciated. Immediately the energy she was transmitting changed completely. I taught her how to reactivate this feeling outside of hypnosis, and asked her to call back in a week. Initially I taught her how to reactivate the feeling of being loved and relaxed for just thirty minutes at a time so she could compare the effect with her anxiety. Within a week she had had so many positive experiences her anxiety had totally faded away.

I was asked to see a young man for an American TV show about social confidence. He was a nice guy with a wry sense of humour and a lovely warm heart. However, he felt he was so worthless that he looked as though he was embarrassed to exist. Unconsciously he was transmitting a message that said, 'Please don't look at me.' When he talked he avoided eye contact. When he stood up his shoulders were hunched and when he spoke he hesitated and mumbled. He wanted to know what to do to attract women. He had no idea that his internal feelings, his posture and his lack of eye contact were all sending out powerful signals that he was not open to a relationship.

I showed him the exercises in the next section and he felt different in a few minutes. And when he felt different on the inside he transformed his effect on people around him on the outside. He went out that night and he got phone numbers from three different women. He still felt a little nervous when he asked them, but he went ahead and asked because he felt so much more comfortable being himself.

Many people have told me that they 'self-sabotage' as though there is some strange part of their brain that randomly undermines their actions and they have no control over it. Well, I guess there may be someone out there like that. But every time I have worked with people who say they 'self-sabotage' I have discovered that hidden beneath their behaviour is fear. They are frightened of something, normally of getting hurt, of getting it wrong or getting punished. Those fears block them from going forward. The next exercises completely remove the power of those fears.

## How to stop holding yourself back

Years ago a mobile telephone was the size of brick and all it could do was make phone calls. Now it is smaller than a bar of chocolate and you can use it to watch TV. In the same period of time there have been astonishing advances in psychological technology. Years ago it took six months to remove a phobia. Now if a therapist takes more than sixty minutes they should be embarrassed.

One of the most exciting recent developments is the massive breakthrough in removing blocks and debilitating feelings. The technique I am about to show you originally came from military research used to remove trauma. I believe it is the greatest advance in psychological treatment in the last fifty years.

This technique was developed by my good friend Dr Ruden. The accurate scientific name is Amygdala Depotentiation Techniques (ADT) but it has become known more simply as 'havening'. Havening delinks thoughts from feelings. The process is so deceptively simple you will almost not believe that it works but Dr Ruden and I have been using it for several years now with almost miraculous results.

## A major scientific breakthrough

In a traumatic situation, a part of the brain called the amygdala releases a neurotransmitter that is captured by means of a receptor called the AMPA receptor. This passes on the message to release the fight-or-flight response. When the message has been delivered, the AMPA receptor is reabsorbed, which effectively 'closes the door' and stops any further arousal.

Dr Ruden's hypothesis is that if a person experiences a trauma as inescapable, then this process is modified.

Phosphorus is also released, which glues the AMPA receptor to the surface of the receiving neuron. This is a bit like jamming the door open so whenever the person experiences something similar to the initial trauma, the fight-or-flight response is triggered instantly. This is the post-traumatic stress response.

Havening cures this by evoking the memory of the initial trauma but simultaneously inducing delta waves, which removes the phosphorus that was gluing the AMPA receptors on the surface of the receiving neurons, thus allowing them to be reabsorbed. This effectively 'closes the door' and stops the repetition of the traumatic response.

The delta waves are generated by gently stroking the upper arms. These soothing gestures mimic the way in which a mother calms and reassures a frightened baby. Her gestures ensure that even though a baby may be scared, the fear leaves no lasting trace. After just one session of havening, people can remember all the factual details of the traumatic events in their past but the associated emotional distress has been removed.

If you would like to explore the scientific background of havening in greater depth please visit www.havening.org.

I recently worked with a woman who had lost her husband after decades of happy marriage. He had passed away the year before and she was inconsolable. After I had worked with her for just twenty minutes she reported that her memories were the same and she missed her husband but she was no longer overwhelmed by the pain of grief.

A little later I worked with a nurse who had had a

successful operation for breast cancer but was terrified that the disease would recur. In twenty minutes her terror was gone. She felt she could relax and enjoy her good health, but she did tell me that she was a bit worried that her overwhelming fear would return. We worked for another ten minutes and that worry was removed as well. Havening really is that simple and that quick. Yet it is extraordinarily effective.

Research is still continuing into both the science of havening and its practical applications. I recently worked with Dr Ruden and others on a pre-trial study at Kings College, London to assess the effect of havening on post-traumatic stress disorder. The study showed that 70 per cent of the subjects could overcome a major trauma with just one session of havening. The remaining 30 per cent also achieved a major benefit, although the improvement was spread over a few more sessions.

## Getting the edge

One of our colleagues on the Kings College study was Deborah Tom, a chartered occupational psychologist with many contacts in the field of coaching. She realized that havening did not need to be confined to the remedial context. She could use it to remove obstacles that hold people back. Now coaches all over the world are using it to bring their clients to peak performance.

My experience with clients, even some inhabitants of Hollywood who are already very successful and famous, is that many of us are inhibited about being truly powerful. Some people are reluctant to be seen as big, bright or powerful. Many cover this up by pretending they don't really want that much success, or they claim they don't want the responsibility of leadership.

Some of those who actually do have power are secretly frightened that one day people will 'see through' them and find out that they are frauds. Others have constructed an entire personality behind which they hide their true selves. Some famous actors have told me that deep down they are extremely shy and they became actors because they had spent so much time learning to hide behind an act of confidence.

## Havening and influence

I have been truly amazed at how so much positive change can be induced so swiftly by havening, and Dr Ruden and I are continuing to find new applications for this technique. For example, practical experimentation has revealed that chanting therapeutic statements during the havening procedure amplifies their impact. Physical conditions such as rosacea have been cured by the repetition of healing statements during havening. It seems that havening can amplify the influence of intention on our own physical state.

Most recently we have successfully combined the knowledge about the workings of the unconscious mind which we have gathered from hypnosis with the therapeutic effects of havening.

This has enabled us to treat blocks which exist in our unconscious even when they are so deeply buried that we cannot consciously access the details of their content or origin.

This is fantastically useful, because many of us simply don't know what was causing our problems or inhibitions. Far too many people have the experience of freezing up under pressure, turning away from challenges or failing to seize opportunities but they simply don't know why. Now we don't need to seek the original cause. We can use the unconscious mind to track down the blocks and then apply the power of havening to remove them.

## Haven away the blocks

I would like to show you how you can use havening to remove those limiting beliefs and free yourself to be completely at ease with your natural power and dignity. I want to show you personally myself, right now, so you can see exactly how to do it. Play the video download and watch the havening section now.

When you have watched it through and accompanied me as I do it, you will be able to do this process on your own. I have written it out below for reference for those times when you cannot refer to the download. However, please use the download first, before using the instructions below, so that you can see precisely how to do it and so that I can take you through each stage personally myself.

## HAVENING

*Remember, please use the download first.*

1.  Think of a time when you wanted to be powerful or successful but were stopped by an inner block or feeling.

2.  Now, cross your arms as though you are hugging yourself, so that your right hand is resting at the top of your left upper arm and your left hand is at the top of your right upper arm.

3.  Gently but firmly stroke your hands down your upper arms. When you reach your elbows lift your hands up and stroke down again from the top of your upper arms.

4.  Continue this motion for the duration of this exercise.

5.  Now imagine walking down a flight of stairs and in your mind count the stairs, from one to ten, all the time continuing to stroke your upper arms gently.

6.  When you reach the bottom of the stairs, continue the stroking and continue to remember that time and say to yourself, 'I am free to be powerful and successful.'

7.  Repeat the statement 'I am free to be powerful and successful' every 10 seconds over and over again for 1 minute, while continuing the havening movement.

8.  When you have finished, check that your base feeling has changed. If the change is not yet sufficient, repeat steps 3 to 7 until you are confident that the limiting belief has been eliminated or is so weak that it is unimportant. If you wish, you can do this over several sessions.

*Havening is not just remedial. We can use havening to enhance your increasing power and influence. When you have done the preceding exercise so much that the old block has vanished or become unimportant, you can move on to the exercise below.*

1. Imagine seeing yourself like a character in a movie in a situation where you need to be influential, confident or powerful – for example, dealing with a volatile teenager, handling a difficult customer, asking an attractive person out on a date, making a speech or closing a deal. Imagine your particular situation going just the way you want it to and reaching a really positive conclusion.

2. Watch the movie a couple of times then start the havening motion as in the above exercise: cross your arms as though you were hugging yourself so that your right hand is resting at the top of your left upper arm and your left hand is at the top of your right upper arm.

3. Gently but firmly stroke your hands down your upper arms. When you reach your elbows, lift your hands up and stroke down again from the top of your upper arms.

4. Now imagine walking down a flight of stairs and in your mind count the stairs, from 1 to 10, all the time continuing to stroke your upper arms gently.

5. Next look again at the movie you created and imagine floating into the scene and seeing through your own eyes as it goes just the way you want it to. Notice your own internal state as you feel influential, confident and powerful. Continue with this feeling for at least 1 minute.

6.  Do this as often as you wish until it begins to feel very natural to feel influential, confident and powerful.

## Why this system works

Everything we do affects how we are, so our state of being is in a continual process of feedback.

We now know that posture affects our feelings and vice versa. We know that how we talk to ourselves affects our self-esteem. Our internal state is the result of the constant interaction of posture, behaviour, physiology, emotions and cognition.

We can illustrate it like this. All these elements contribute to our state of being. Wherever we intervene it will have an effect on all the other elements in the circle.

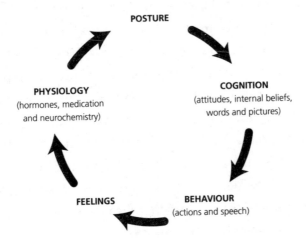

Amy Cuddy's power poses affect our physiology and hence our behaviour and feelings and cognition. The exercise of transforming your internal voice intervenes at the level of cognition, and from there affects everything else. Similarly havening and orthodox pharmaceutical medicines intervene at the level of physiology and affect the other elements from there.

There are many ways we can make use of this feedback loop, both in ourselves and in others. Crucially, we can intervene at any point in the circle. Wherever we intervene the effect will spread all around the circle. For example, my friend Robert Holden devised a process which I described in *I Can Make You Happy*, which has been proven to elevate the mood of depressed people. He prescribes three things: exercise, laughter and positive thoughts. These interventions, two at the level of behaviour and one at the level of cognition, change all the other elements including physiology and feelings. It doesn't matter if people have to fake the laughter at first. Robert asks his clients to put coloured dots around the house and to force themselves to think of something positive each time they see a dot. Over time this repetition of thoughts causes the corresponding neural networks to become physically bigger in the brain. Robert's process had such a remarkably positive effect that when the BBC made a programme about it they could not believe initially that the effects would last. They delayed transmission of the programme for six months to make sure that Robert's subjects maintained their improvement. They did so, and the programme was broadcast.

We can all make huge changes in our capacity to influence other people by adjusting our attitudes. Attitudes are simply patterns of thought and perspective which predispose us to particular feelings.

## The power of optimism

Our internal state continually affects all those around us, so any attitude which affects that state will be very influential. The single most powerful attitude I know is optimism. One of my favourite pieces of psychological research shows us just how powerful it is.

Some time ago researchers conducted a survey to discover what sort of psychotherapeutic treatment was actually effective. They interviewed a number of clients who affirmed that psychotherapy had worked for them, and then they interviewed their therapists and asked them what they had done. The therapists reported using a wide variety of different techniques and interventions. The clients, however, explained the success very differently. They didn't talk much about techniques or interventions. In fact, the single most common cause offered for success was simple: the client felt that the psychotherapist believed in them. It was the optimistic attitude of the therapist that lead the client to be successful. Across the whole sample, the attitude of optimism was more effective than any other intervention.

Another study looked at the effect of optimism in politics. Looking at the United States, one of the largest democratic electorates in the world, researchers assessed the optimism of candidates in ten presidential elections. In nine out of ten elections the most optimistic candidate won. Optimism is a crucial component of success.

## The easy way to increase optimism

Optimism is the most functional basis for influence, because whatever you intend will be reinforced by your optimism. Persuasion and persistence are both supported and maintained by optimism. When you know that things will work out in your favour, it is much easier to keep going. Optimism creates a virtuous circle of self-reinforcement.

Strangely, optimism can be even stronger when it is vague. You don't need to know how things will work out. But optimism will keep you going until they do. Optimism is very, very simple but it has a radical impact on success.

Real optimism breeds real success. Remember, however, that human beings are pretty good at spotting a fake – and fake optimism is off-putting. Don't pretend to feel hopeful or happy. Do all the exercises above thoroughly until you genuinely, naturally see positive possibilities whatever your situation. Your power to influence will become stronger and stronger as your own success day by day reinforces your optimism.

Even when things look difficult, or the situation is painful, challenging or even tragic, a fundamental attitude of optimism will help you and the people around you to move towards improvement. You don't have to be happy to be optimistic. You could be sad or lonely or angry and yet still be optimistic because you know that sooner or later things will improve and you will feel better.

We can all be optimistic. So, right now, I'd like you to rate your own optimism. On a scale of 0 to 10 where 0 is none at all and 10 is as much as possible, how optimistic are you? At this stage I don't need you to be super accurate, just give yourself a quick approximate rating.

If you registered 10, congratulations! You are well on your way to being a phenomenally successful influencer. If you rated any number less than 10, the following exercises are for you.

## THE OPTIMISM CONTEXT

*My friend and colleague Michael Neill created this method to make a positive context for challenges.*

1. Think of an issue you face that you believe to be difficult, depressing or challenging.

2. Notice how you feel.

3. Now, imagine a huge square in front of you cut into nine screens, like a noughts-and-crosses board, with three rows of three.

4. Leave the one in the middle of the bottom row empty.

5. Fill the other screens one by one with pictures of times you felt really good about yourself or about life – for example, laughing with a friend, seeing a beautiful sunset, falling in love, playing a game, winning a prize, helping someone and feeling good, walking on a beach and so on.

6. Make all those pictures bright, clear and beautiful.

7. When all the other squares are full, place the challenging issue in the box in the middle of the bottom row.

8. Notice how much better you feel about that issue now.

The next exercise trains your mind to remember that even in the worst of times good things happen. When you are living life it can feel random and painful, but when you look back you can see what you learned. We can't remove all the tough times from our lives but we can move through them better and more quickly. I encourage you to add optimism to your life, but also to be grateful for what you learn by getting through the challenges.

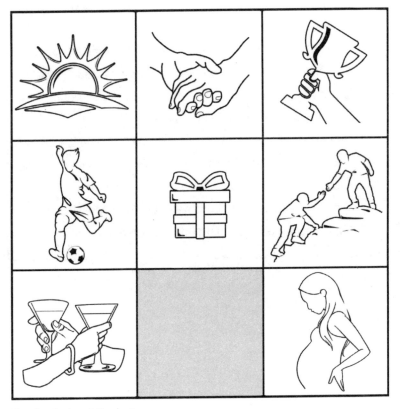

The Optimism Mindset

## THE OPTIMISM MINDSET

1.  Think of three things that have gone wrong for you in the last month – however large or small. Perhaps you dropped something, or lost something or failed to receive something you were hoping for. Whatever they were, write them down now.

2.  Now write down next to them a benefit to you that happened because of that thing that went wrong. Again, it doesn't matter whether it is large or small – and it doesn't have to match the thing that went wrong. For example, a car accident might be a very negative experience and the positive experience of consequently missing a boring meeting at work is not at all comparable – but nevertheless it would be a benefit. If it happened, write it down.

3.  Hereafter, whenever something negative happens, look for the benefits, however small, which also follow from the same event. The point is not to deny difficulty, danger or sadness, but to train ourselves to become aware that, however difficult life is, there is always a path open towards a better situation.

# IN A NUTSHELL

- You are continually influencing people

- Your own state is your most powerful tool of influence

- Increasing your optimism increases your influence

# NEXT STEPS

➤ Practise power poses

➤ Banish negative self-talk

➤ Use a confident external voice

➤ Haven away blocks

➤ Increase your optimism

# 3
.
# HOW TO GET PEOPLE TO LIKE AND TRUST YOU

# How to get people to like and trust you

By the time you finish this book you will find that you can wield enormous influence in the shortest conversations. Sometimes a single remark is enough. Several times people have said to me, 'Thank you so much for your help', and I have no recollection at all of doing anything to help. Then they tell me that they vividly remember a single phrase in a short exchange a few years ago which completely changed their lives.

I used to think that getting people to do things would be difficult, but as I accessed the goldmine of information in this system I found that it has become easier and easier.

# How to get people to trust you

Scientific research shows that we are more inclined to agree with people if we like them. People tend to like people who are similar to themselves, so we find ways to be similar to the people we want to influence. This is known as gaining rapport.

The key to rapport is reducing difference and increasing similarity, while at the same time being true to our own natures. To gain rapport with a given individual we amplify what we have in common with that person. I like to think of building rapport as being natural and true to myself, but also giving an extra nudge to friendliness.

The most sound basis for rapport is physiology. When you align your physiology with another person they sense it at an unconscious level and feel at ease with you. If you shift your posture, your gestures and the speed of your movement so that it is more like that of the other person, you are sending a signal direct to their unconscious mind that you are similar to them and therefore trustworthy.

If someone has a firm handshake, make your handshake firm too. If someone stands or sits in a very upright position you too can become a little more upright. If someone is lively and using a lot of gestures, allow your own body to be a bit more expressive too. You don't need to copy their gestures; just using your own gestures with the same sort of size or pace will deliver a signal to their unconscious that you are similar, because you too are physically expressive.

This is what people do naturally when they like each other. For example, when you are walking with a friend you naturally fall into step with them.

## The science of rapport

In the 1990s scientists in Italy discovered that monkeys' brains responded in the same way when they saw an action as when they did it themselves. They called the neurons that behave like this 'mirror neurons'.

Further research has indicated that mirror neurons exist in humans too. Researchers demonstrate that in humans the same part of the brain reacts both to the sight of someone being touched and to being touched themselves.

Other research shows that this is also the mechanism by which the brain interprets and reacts to facial expressions. So when you see a smile, the 'smiling' part of your own brain is stimulated, hence you feel that same smiling feeling. Mirror neurons respond to intention as well as action. In one experiment subjects saw a person pick up a cup from a table for three different reasons: once to drink in the context of a party, once to clear the table after a party, and once with no context at all. A different pattern of mirror activity was observed on each occasion. Communications professionals have known about rapport from empirical evidence for many years. It is exciting that now neuroscientists are able to identify the precise mechanism by which it works.

## The great misunderstanding about rapport

Some people have misunderstood rapport as copying people. People do not generally like to be copied. If they feel they are being imitated or mimicked they feel mocked. That creates active dislike and breaks rapport in such a way that makes it difficult to regain. When people try to get rapport like this it just feels creepy. It is another reason why sales people with old-school training can be so off-putting.

Genuine physiological rapport is far more gentle and subtle than blatant imitation. There is absolutely no need to copy gestures or movement, because your aim is simply to reduce differences, not to replicate behaviour. The communications of the unconscious mind are infinitely subtle and cannot be reduced to a mimicry. Similarly 'body language' is a simplistic reductionist code in which folded arms are interpreted as 'very confident' or 'closed to new ideas' or 'very cold'.

## Physiology the most powerful key to trust

To gain rapport, start with physiology. To begin with, notice the overall speed at which a person is moving or talking and speed up or slow down yourself so that you reduce the difference between you. There is no need to try to 'match' them exactly, just to move a bit closer. Notice their overall level of tension and, again, reduce the differences between you.

If they are moving or gesticulating, do not try to imitate them. If they lean forward and cross their arms, do not do the same. You will just look strange. Instead you could just interlace your fingers. In other words you reflect a movement in one area with a similar movement somewhere else. This is called 'crossover mirroring'. There is no need for anyone to notice it at a conscious level. It works directly at the level of the unconscious mind.

If someone is tapping their feet, don't imitate them. However, you could just tap your finger a few times in time with them. If someone is making a big gesture with their arm, you could increase your similarity by a slight inclination of your head every third or fourth time.

You can build rapport at a distance by crossover mirroring. If, for example, I wish to build rapport with someone else at a dinner table when they take a drink, I just touch my glass or my lips. I don't do this slavishly every time; two or three times out of four. Minimal, intermittent crossover mirroring is more natural and therefore more effective.

As you practise and experiment with this, don't start big. Start by doing as little as you can, then one day it will click and the world of influence will open up for you at another level. What seemed like magic will become obvious and you will find it as simple and easy as smiling and laughing.

You can play with these ideas a lot and have fun being inventive but don't get too carried away. Remember, people do like similarity but generally they don't like people who try so hard to be like others that they stop being true to themselves.

You can practise this sort of rapport any time you want. Do it in a very small way. If someone thinks you are copying them you have failed. The best type of physical rapport is minimal and all the more effective because it is not registered at the level of conscious awareness.

After the initial stage of practising, creating rapport should not feel like hard work. We naturally create rapport with our friends without any conscious effort. Good rapport is effortless.

## RAPPORT EXERCISE 1

*Try this exercise when you meet a stranger in a neutral public space, such as on public transport, in a shop or at the gym. All you need to start is to ask an open question. An open question is one to which the answer cannot be 'yes' or 'no'. For example, 'How did you hear about this shop?' This exercise is really a game to practise and ratify rapport.*

1. Say hi and ask an open question.

2. Carry on the conversation.

3. Gradually, increase the similarity between their posture and your own.

4. Now, gradually allow your speech to become a little more similar to theirs.

5. Do some minimal crossover rapport – for example, tap your finger every third time someone touches their face.

6. After five or ten minutes, make a small addition to your crossover rapport – for example, as you tap your finger, scratch the back of your hand and see if the other person adds a similar gesture to their unconscious actions.

# The hidden power of words

According to one famous research study, when you talk to someone, 55 per cent – over half – of all that is understood is carried by your physiology, your breathing, posture, gesture, muscle tonus, skin tone, facial expressions and movement. Much of this is driven by your internal state, so you will increase your rapport by moving towards the emotional state of the person to whom you are talking. We cannot help but pick up on each other's emotional states.

You can also use crossover mirroring. I sometimes match the rise and fall of a client's breathing with an infinitesimal rise and fall in the pitch or volume of my speech.

Another 38 per cent of your meaning – approximately one-third – is conveyed not by your words but by your vocal qualities. The tone, speed, volume and inflections of your words convey more than five times as much as the actual words. For example, the smallest word can have a multitude of very, very different meanings:

Yes      (flat tone, I agree)

YES!     (louder and with enthusiasm, I very much agree)

Yeeees   (I am unsure but curious)

Yes      (upward inflection meaning confused)

Yes      (upward inflection meaning sceptical)

Yess     (lower tone conveying satisfaction)

There are hundreds of ways to say yes. The tone conveys far, far more than the word. Tone is just one of many opportunities to increase rapport. You can increase similarity with someone else's speech by using any of its variables. You make your tone, rhythm, timbre and inflections closer to the speech you hear. Once again, I emphasize that there is no value in attempting to exactly match someone.

The tone conveys the emotional state of the speaker so you can also move yourself towards that state. You can reduce difference by simply getting a bit closer to their speed, volume and patterns of speech. If I tend to speak more slowly than you, you can increase our similarity by speaking a little more slowly. If my voice is quieter than yours, you will build rapport by speaking more quietly yourself. Again, you can use crossover mirroring, matching speed of speech with a minimal gesture, or matching loudness with the size of your physical movement.

## The core of every relationship: values

Finally, when you talk, 7 per cent of what you are communicating is conveyed by your words. In that 7 per cent you clarify the facts, beliefs and values you are communicating.

The key to building rapport is to discover values. When you know someone's values you know what to share of your own and you know a great deal about their perspective on life. Ultimately your decision about whether to trust someone or work with someone must be based on your understanding of their values.

When I meet someone new I usually explore two topics. The first is to find out what or whom we have in common. Have we been to the same places, do we have friends in common, have we read the same books or do we share an interest? Anything we share can foster rapport.

The second thing I do is to seek out whatever that person is passionate about. When people talk about their passions they are more energetic and they want to share their interest. Someone's passion will reveal what they value.

## The power to move people where you want

Our words may contain only 7 per cent of what we communicate but they offer many opportunities to reduce differences and enhance similarities. In particular the metaphors we choose illustrate the ways we prefer to think. In general people tend to favour one of three different styles: visual, auditory or kinaesthetic. These different ways of thinking affect how we speak, how we process ideas and our preferences in the world. They also tend to affect our speech. People tend to favour metaphors which reflect their sensory preferences.

People who favour visual metaphors tend to explain themselves by painting pictures in the mind. They might talk about blue-sky thinking, clarity of vision, and seeing past black-and-white divisions into a more colourful palette of possibilities. You will demonstrate your understanding if you think and express yourself visually too. You could talk about shining a light on issues and drawing conclusions from a common perspective.

People who favour auditory metaphors may talk about how an idea rings a bell or resonates with them. They may talk about achieving harmony or sounding out possibilities. Things they like are music to their ears.

Kinaesthetic refers to physical feeling and such people tend to use concrete, physical metaphors. They talk about building bridges, standing firm, reaching out and overcoming obstacles. If you hear phrases like that you could use a few concrete metaphors yourself. You could talk about creating solid foundations and pulling together to form a robust team.

It is great fun to play with metaphors and in particular to experiment with the styles with which you are least familiar. When you do that, you increase your verbal dexterity and your capacity to build rapport more quickly with a larger number of people.

Metaphors and styles of expression form a huge and fertile field for rapport. I mention them here briefly, but you could usefully spend weeks exploring and experimenting. When you use the same type of metaphors as someone else, you also get an insight into their thinking, so building rapport will also foster mutual understanding.

You will find that people tend to end up with jobs or

hobbies that match their natural affinities. In my experience, TV directors and interior designers are overwhelming visual. Sound guys favour auditory metaphors and are great at assessing people's characters just by listening to their voices. You will also notice that people's values and interests are reflected in the language and metaphors they use. Competitive people use metaphors of battle and conflict. Sports fans use sporting metaphors. Homemakers use metaphors of building and furnishing. All of these provide more opportunities for reducing difference.

I introduced the idea of rapport in the first book I published about hypnosis. My editor read it and went over to the office of one of her colleagues with whom she didn't get on particularly well. In those days understanding of rapport was very basic and she simply tried to match his posture and physiology. Then as she talked to him she gradually shifted her speech to match his speed and tone and she used crossover mirroring to get in sync with his gestures. After a few minutes, she scratched her head, and he immediately did the same thing. A little later she scratched her head again, and he did it again. A while later she did it a third time, and so did he. She burst out laughing and had to leave his office. She called me and could hardly stop laughing as she told me about it. She couldn't believe that she could affect someone so quickly.

## The power of self-awareness

In order to make any of these changes you have to be aware of the characteristics of your own natural speech. Some of us can be very unaware of our own patterns. We are so used to them that we pay them no attention. I sometimes suggest to my clients that they record a few minutes of video of themselves talking about a pet subject and then play it back. The view from the outside can help you be objective about the characteristics of your speech. Quite a few have reported back that they didn't realize how loudly they spoke, or how much they hesitated or mumbled.

I suggest you make a quick video of yourself too. One or two minutes is all you need.

Watch the video and use as many adjectives as you can to describe your own speech. It could be, for example, lively, passionate, gentle, firm, quick, relaxed, laid-back, warm, precise, humorous or one of a hundred other characteristics.

Now you know a little more about your own default settings, there will be some characteristics which are particularly salient. This is your baseline. When you want to build rapport, you know where you are most different from your target and therefore where you can most easily reduce differences.

Now, watch or think about a few of your acquaintances. In which ways are they similar to you, and in which ways are they different? If, for example, you notice that you tend to have the loudest voice in the room, you know that it is likely you will have to speak more quietly to build rapport with strangers. If you tend to sound serious, you could practise being more light-hearted. That doesn't mean you suddenly have to crack jokes or become a comedian. It could be just a matter of allowing your tone of voice to move towards being gently amused.

As you practise your skills of rapport and influence, you will find it useful from time to time to do another video. The key to improving your own abilities swiftly is to compare yourself to your previous self. You give yourself a benchmark, you can measure progress and, as your skill and acuity increases, you will notice more details and more modalities in which to practise rapport.

## CREATING RAPPORT 2

*In a neutral public space such as on public transport, in a shop or meeting someone for the first time, build rapport using multiple variables.*

1.  In conversation with someone, notice their posture and gesture.
2.  Gradually and minimally change your own posture and gestures towards the style the other person has.
3.  Listen for the metaphors they are using.
4.  Notice if they are mostly visual, auditory or kinaesthetic.
5.  Introduce a few metaphors of the same modality into your own speech.

## Creating a deeper feeling of affinity

Whenever you meet people there are countless opportunities for rapport. I have just introduced the subject here with some of the central methods, but you can find many, many more. All the variables of speech, gesture and presence offer the possibility of building rapport.

We also know, more prosaically, that we warm to people who share our ideas or interests. I do not recommend pretending or attempting to change your views to match everyone you meet. The outcome will be confusing for you and unsettling for others. Furthermore, it won't work, because the fact that you keep changing will be more salient than whatever you are changing to.

Every now and then you will find that you meet people who get on really well but seem to have very different styles of speech and behaviour. For example, you might meet a very loud and brash woman whose husband says very little, yet they seem in perfect rapport. This may seem to be a counter-example. However, you will find that even though the exteriors do not match, they are complementary, and what the couple actually share is an identical set of values. In their value set the woman does the public relations and the man is the thinker in the background.

When you are seeking rapport, keep a very, very open mind and find out if there are areas of interest, or views, opinions or ideas that you do share with someone. For example, your political views may be quite different but you could share a passion for cookery or sport.

## Dealing with difficult people

The more we have rapport, the more we influence each other. That means that if I have established good rapport, I can change another person's mood by the process of changing my own.

A few years ago a dear friend of mine, whose career has been so successful he has more than enough of all the luxuries in life, was having a very bad time. A number of serious events had gone against him, a relationship had broken down and a deal had fallen through. A mutual friend rang me sounding very alarmed. He told me he was frightened that our friend would do something stupid. He asked me to go over there. I drove straight over and banged on his door for ten minutes before he would let me in. He was in a furious rage. He had had far too much to drink, he was angry with everyone and he was threatening to do lots of very stupid things, including even killing himself. So I got angry. I didn't get angry at him. I got angry with him. I also began swearing and raging about all the selfish, cheating bastards in town, about all the corporate clones who didn't care about talent and all the women who were manipulative schemers. And about the men who didn't give a damn about stealing your money or your women. I shared his fury and then I got a bit tired and calmed down a little. Then he got angry again and I got angry again too. I swore and shouted and slammed the table. Then I paused a bit and he paused a bit. Then we got angry again and a little calmer again. When he fired up again, I joined him in the anger and then gradually drifted towards being calmer and he drifted with me. And over about two hours we ranted and raged together and got exhausted together and little by little got quieter and quieter, each time for a little bit longer. Eventually we ended up having a long, serious talk about the issues he was facing.

## The magical effects of pace and lead

The process I used is known as 'pace and lead'. You get into rapport with someone by reducing differences and increasing similarities. You start with physiology and you match their emotional energy. Then you match tone and finally some elements of the content of what they are saying.

Then gradually you change your own emotional state. Because you are now in rapport, by changing yourself you bring them with you. You can do this gently but often you can do it amazingly fast. It rarely takes as long as it took me with my distraught friend. In that case the fact that he was drunk as well as angry meant that he was less in control of himself, so it took longer to calm him down. Whatever the situation, the key is not to rush and to make sure that your emotional transition feels natural to you so it can also feel natural to them. I think of the process as like pulling someone with a thread of cotton. I must be careful not to pull too hard and break the cotton, but if I pull very gently, little by little they will respond.

Pace and lead is a useful and versatile method of influence when people are in extreme states of emotion. You don't need to have any clever arguments or knowledge about what is disturbing them. All you need to do is match their emotional state and energy as you talk to them and each time you speak slightly reduce your own level of energy.

Pace and lead can be used in many situations. It is not just about extreme drama. The basic principle is: 'If you want someone to do something, do it yourself.' If you want them to talk about their brother, talk about your brother. If you want them to get happy, get happy yourself.

## HOW TO PACE AND LEAD

1. Ensure you are in a resourceful and flexible state (by using exercises from Chapter 2).

2. Observe the other person.

3. Gain rapport by reducing differences and increasing similarities.

4. Gradually change your own state while maintaining rapport.

5. If necessary, change your state gradually and retreat a little from time to time, taking two steps forward and one back.

## Polarity responders

I can guarantee that sooner or later you will meet someone with whom it all goes wrong. You work hard at building rapport but just as soon as you feel you are getting somewhere, the other person takes off in the opposite direction. Or you are working together on a problem and you make a promising suggestion but, before you get a chance to explore it, the other person dismisses it and suggests the complete opposite. Whatever you propose, they propose the opposite.

There are people to whom this contrariness comes naturally. They can be very creative and inventive thinkers. They can also be extremely irritating. They are polarity responders.

Polarity responders have a tendency to reject whatever is present and argue the opposing point of view. It may be that they are plagued by low self-esteem and feel the need to assert themselves by disagreeing with everyone. Often it is a habit so ingrained that they are unaware of it themselves. Regardless of the cause, the key to influencing and working with polarity responders is to recognize their pattern and adjust your own behaviour. When you are getting to know someone and building rapport, be alert for signs that they favour disagreement. If you are in doubt, offer a few opinions and observe their response. Do they start by disagreeing or correcting you? Do they say, 'Yes but . . .'?

My little godson was going through a phase of being a polarity responder. I wanted a photo with him and his mother so I told him to get out of the way so I could photograph her alone. 'Why?' he asked. I told him I just wanted to photograph his mum, but he insisted on pushing into the photo. I got the photo I needed. His mother was delighted. 'Now I know what to do!' she said. I told her it would work for a couple of weeks before he cottoned on, then she would have to revise her strategy.

If you identify a polarity responder you must learn to hold back the opinion you really wish to advance and start somewhere else. You must also learn to be patient and not to get angry at what seems to be gratuitous contrariness. This can be difficult at first, but it just takes practice. You don't have to say the total opposite of what you want, but make sure you begin with something quite distant from your true wishes. With practice you will find that polarity is just as easy to use as agreement or pacing and leading. You just push a bit in the opposite direction to where you want to go. After a while you will get good at making polarity responders believe they have created the suggestions you desire.

# IN A NUTSHELL

- Rapport is about reducing differences and increasing similarities

- Self-awareness increases your flexibility

- Polarity responders are predictable

# NEXT STEPS

➤ Get to know your own default settings

➤ Practise building rapport with variables of speech, posture and gesture

➤ Practise pace and lead

# 4

.

# THE HOT BUTTONS
# OF HUMAN BEINGS

## The hot buttons of human beings

Human beings carry out thousands of complex activities every day, from making a cup of tea to driving a car, without thinking about all the intricate motor actions we are performing. We don't have to decide what to do over and over again because we have a wonderful capacity to learn something and then repeat it automatically. When you were a child, you learned how to open a door. After just a few goes your brain generalized your learning so that you know how to open a door everywhere. If this didn't happen, you would have to figure it out each time you came to a door. This learning is a combination of automation and generalization. It is as though we have an autopilot which will switch on as soon as it recognizes the situation.

This is amazingly useful but, as you will see, it is also the gateway to a range of fantastically powerful routes of influence. Effectively people have built-in hot buttons which drive automatic responses. You will learn how to press those buttons to deliver the results you require.

## Automation

My friend Robert Cialdini, the pre-eminent social psychologist, has produced a masterly overview of the automatic patterns that humans use to run their lives in his excellent book,

*Influence, Science and Practice.* Professor Cialdini suggests that our capacity to automate is an evolution of the fixed-action patterns that drive animal behaviour.

In turkeys, for example, the instinct of mothering is triggered by the cheeping noise of young turkey chicks. That is all it takes. The appearance or scent of the chicks seems to be of little or no relevance. If the chick makes the *cheep cheep* sound, the turkey will mother it. If it does not make the right sound, the mother will ignore it, or even kill it.

Animal behaviourist Michael W. Fox demonstrated the overriding power of this fixed-action pattern by putting a little tape-recorder playing the *cheep cheep* sound inside a stuffed polecat. The polecat is a natural enemy of the turkey, but the mother turkey still mothered it. The moment the *cheep cheep* was turned off, the turkey attacked it.

The difference between us and other animals is that we can learn new patterns and we can change the ones we have learned. The similarity is that we use automatic patterns of behaviour throughout our lives.

We can automate at every level of our existence. We automate motor skills, like walking, writing and tying shoelaces. We automate cognitive skills like language use, recognition and interpretation. We automate social skills like shaking hands, flirting and dancing. These automatic skills are like habits, and we can combine and run lots of them simultaneously.

We create our own habits to run our daily lives. Each of us tends to start the day with our own particular routine of washing, dressing and breakfast. If you drive a car to work you don't think consciously about every movement of your arms or legs, or about changing gear or indicating or using your rear-view mirror. You engage your autopilot and you are free to listen to the radio or have a conversation with your passengers.

## Automatic thinking

We use this capacity to automate in our thinking too. Some of us like to imagine that we direct our lives with rational, conscious decisions, but even if we do so sometimes, much of the time we run on autopilot.

Our brains recognize patterns around us, so instead of using up energy analysing what looks like the situation all over again, we automatically make assumptions. Those assumptions can then drive our actions with little if any conscious decision-making at all.

These mental short-cuts are useful and efficient because most of the time our assumptions are correct. That's how they come into existence in the first place. However, the tendency to make these assumptions can be used to influence our behaviour. Equally, you can use it to influence other people's behaviour. In this chapter we will look at the most common and powerful of these patterns of automatic thinking. Robert has identified six major patterns of automatic behaviour. Here we will review them and also show you how each one can be used.

# SOCIAL PROOF

One of the most common drivers of human behaviour is known as 'social proof'. Social proof is simply this: if everyone else is doing it, we assume it is the right thing to do.

The vast majority of what we absorb through social proof is helpful. The ways we do the basics of life are transmitted to us by social proof. We don't have lessons in eating or queueing or shaking hands. We learn them from the people around us. We learn how to speak our native language. We learn the unspoken rules of our own particular society which help us to get along together. We learn to greet each other and work together. We learn about privacy and cooperation. Informal learning like this, via social proof, is very efficient and is a vital precursor to formal learning in schools. Social proof is part of the glue that holds societies together and protects us.

Fashion is the perfect example of social proof. When a certain number of people pick up on a trend it suddenly becomes hot and everyone copies it. Fashion seems quite lightweight, but you can see its power when you imagine someone wearing clothes that are five or ten years out of style. People just don't do it because it would look too out-of-date.

Social proof is powerful even in very small-scale situations. I was in a carriage on the New York subway with about a dozen other people when a beggar got on. I put my hand in my pocket to give him a few dollars, but six people in front of me all turned away and none of them gave the beggar anything. As he came past me, my hand stayed in my pocket. I had been influenced by the six people in front of me.

In a formal psychological experiment subjects were shown patterns of lines. One line was clearly shorter. The subjects were asked the length of that line and one after another the first nine subjects all said it was the same as the others. The tenth subject followed suit. The first nine subjects had all been coached to lie. The behaviour of the tenth subject, the only real subject of the experiment, demonstrated the power of social proof.

Some organizations have used social proof in a blatantly manipulative way. A research team at Arizona University infiltrated the Billy Graham organization and reported on their advance preparations. By the time Graham arrived in town and made his altar call, an army of volunteers were waiting with instructions on when to come forth at varying intervals to create the impression of a spontaneous mass outpouring. They were primed to put twenty- and fifty-dollar bills in the collection plates, thus prompting others to follow their actions and also to donate high-value bills.

Social media now give us a very clear demonstration of the power of social proof. On media such as Instagram and Facebook, if a link has only a small number of views it is unlikely to be viewed or shared further. The vast majority of links posted have very few views. However, if a link gets past a threshold of a few thousand views it becomes more likely that it will be clicked again. If a link has a hundred thousand views it will be clicked thousands more times by people completely unrelated to the first poster or the area in which it originated. The cause of all those extra views is simply the number that shows hundreds of thousands, and then millions, of other people have viewed it. People choose to click just because other people have.

## Using social proof

Social proof is the basis of a vast number of methods of influence. It is very powerful but it is not so powerful that it causes everyone to do the same thing all the time. We are affected by social proof regardless of whether or not we are aware of it. We tend to be more driven by social proof in four types of situation:

1. When we have to choose between many similar options.
2. When we are facing uncertainty.
3. When we observe behaviour by people we identify as similar to ourselves.
4. When we are establishing social norms.

Let's look at situation 1: when we have to choose between many similar options. We can see this on the street every day. Consider how tourists choose restaurants. If there are three restaurants in a street and two are empty and one is full, people will tend to go to the full one. They infer that other people have chosen it, therefore it is the best restaurant. This is why if you are the first patron of a restaurant in the evening you will be offered a table at the front or in the window so that others can see you.

Advertising is an entire industry dedicated to influencing people and social proof is one of its favourite tools. They like to use slogans such as 'Millions sold', 'Bestseller', 'the nation's favourite', 'Number 1', 'most popular', 'Recommended', 'Readers' choice' and a hundred variations of the same theme. All of them boil down to a statement of social proof: lots of other people have bought this thing so you should too.

What about situation 2: when we are facing uncertainty?

If we don't know what to do or where to go, our most common response is to look around and do what everyone else is doing. Professor Cialdini cites a series of experiments in which an accident or emergency scene was staged and passers-by were observed. When it was absolutely clear that someone was injured and needed assistance, they received help 100 per cent of the time. However, when it was not clear whether or not the victim was really in trouble – in other words, when there was uncertainty – the effects of social proof were observed. A single passer-by was still likely to offer help. However, if several people were present it was more likely that none of them would venture to help. Each individual was taking their cues from the others, and as no one was sure what to do they just carried on, and passed by the situation.

On the basis of this research, Cialdini offers some

excellent advice, which I will pass on: if you need help in a busy public space choose an individual and ask them directly for the specific help you need. Don't assume people will help. Cialdini himself had personal experience of this when he was involved in a road accident. He and the other driver were clearly injured, and yet the cars that had stopped around them began to move on. Cialdini realized what was happening and followed his own advice. He pointed directly at one driver and said, 'Call the police,' and to another he said, 'Pull over, we need help.' He received help.

In situation 3, social proof is stronger when we see behaviour of people whom we perceive as similar to ourselves. Social psychologists have conducted many ingenious experiments to demonstrate this truth. However, we do not need to set up experiments to see this phenomenon at work. Real life has shown us that it can be literally deadly.

In the 1970s sociologist David Phillips began to study rates of suicide and accidental death. He found that for two months after the report of a suicide there is an increase in the number of suicides. Sadly, there is an average number of suicides every month, but the increase Phillips observed was in excess of this number. In other words more people killed themselves.

The data that Phillips used was from the 1940s to the 1960s, the days before the internet and before the dominance of television. In those days people received much of their news from newspapers. Phillips was able to show that the increase in suicides only happened in the area where the newspapers which reported it were distributed. Furthermore, in those same areas there was a simultaneous increase in fatal car and aeroplane crashes. It might be a bit far-fetched to think that there was a correlation between the accidents and the initial report of suicide – except for two facts. First, if the original story was of a solitary suicide the increase in car and aeroplane accidents was also of a single fatality. If the original suicide also murdered other people, there was an increase in the number of car and aeroplane accidents which had multiple fatalities. Second, Phillips looked at the age of single-fatality suicides. If the suicide was a young person, the accidental fatalities were of young people. If an older person killed themselves, the accidental fatalities were also of older people.

Troubled and vulnerable people saw a report of suicide by someone similar to themselves and tragically chose to kill themselves as well. Some did so overtly, others made a decision to disguise their actions as an accident. Phillips' research should be required reading for the editors of all channels of news.

Situation 4 is about establishing social norms. Social proof is not, thank goodness, always dangerous. And it doesn't even require us to see or to read about people. Sometimes a jar will do. Almost every café has a tips jar next to the till. You will notice that it usually has quite a few notes and coins in it. That jar is a device to prompt you to give a tip. The money already there indicates that other people have given a tip. The principle of social proof says, 'Look, they've done it, so you should do the same.' That's why the jar is never left empty. At the beginning of the day the staff will put in some money, and even when they take tips out they always leave some behind.

My favourite example of the power of social proof is the newcomer at a classical music concert. Regular classical music fans never clap between the movements of a symphony or a concerto. They wait and clap after the final movement. Every now and then a newcomer starts to clap after the first movement. Then as they realize they are alone they stop. They don't clap after the second movement. They wait until everyone else does and then they join in. That's social proof.

Nightclub owners know all about social proof too. Have you ever queued to get in to a club and then discovered that it was half empty? And then asked yourself, why did they make me queue? The answer is social proof. A line of people trying to get in is physical evidence of popularity. It says, 'Look, other people really want to get in here. You should too!'

## Awareness alone is not protection

Interestingly, social proof is influential even when we recognize that it is being used. As an example, Robert Cialdini cites the use of the pre-recorded sound of people laughing on TV comedy shows. Everyone knows it is fake, and many of us don't want it. However, controlled experiments have demonstrated over and over again that 'canned laughter' causes audiences to laugh longer and more often and to rate the jokes as funnier than audiences watching the same show without the canned laughter. We know that laughter is contagious so there may be other factors at work here, but social proof is definitely included.

## SOCIAL PROOF

*I could fill the rest of this book with examples and variations on the theme of social proof. As we look at other tools of influence you will notice that social proof often makes a contribution. If you are interested in exploring it in more depth you will find many books discussing social proof in minute detail. However, I don't need to list hundreds of examples here. Instead I will ask you do a simple exercise.*

1. Look around you for as many examples as you can see of persuasive people, marketing or advertisements using social proof.

2. Write down at least ten examples each day until you find you are spotting so many that you can't write them all down.

# SCARCITY

One particularly powerful variation of social proof is the power of scarcity. Other things being equal, people will value things that are in short supply over things that are available in abundance. The mental short-cut behind this is the inference that things are in short supply because other people have already taken most of them. Other people value these things so I should too.

Bestselling dating manual *The Rules* teaches women how to turn this piece of automatic thinking to their advantage. It advises women that if a man calls after Wednesday they must tell him they are not available. This makes the chance of a date with them more scarce and therefore more valuable. It also builds anticipation because he will have to wait until at least the following week.

The shopping channel QVC makes a great play of limited stocks of its key offers. Often the presenter will show indicators of sales or say there are big queues on the phone. All of these indicators create a pressure on purchasers to move fast before it is too late.

One of my favourite experiments demonstrating the power of scarcity was devised by psychologist Stephen Worchel. He asked people to take part in what he called a 'consumer preference study'. Participants were given a chocolate-chip cookie from a jar and asked to grade its taste and quality. For some of the participants the jar contained ten cookies, for others it contained only two cookies. The cookies from the jar containing only two were rated as more delicious and better quality. Worchel then tweaked the experiment with a further variable. In some cases, participants were shown a jar with ten cookies, then they were told the researcher had made a mistake and it was taken away and returned with two cookies inside. These cookies were rated as even more delicious and desirable. In some other cases, the participants were shown the jar with ten cookies and told that the cookies were needed for other participants before the jar was returned with just two cookies. In these cases the cookies were given the highest rating of deliciousness and quality.

Scarcity is motivating. Items that are scarce are desirable. Items that have recently become more scarce are more desirable. Items that have become more scarce because other people want them are most desirable of all.

Worchel's lesson wasn't lost on me. When I was performing my stage show in the West End of London we found that a simple change in the wording of the advertising posters made a noticeable difference to ticket sales. Originally the posters said 'Paul McKenna's Hypnotic Show, Sundays at the Dominion Theatre'. I wasn't entirely happy with the wording. We changed it to 'Paul McKenna's Hypnotic Show at the Dominion Theatre: 5 Sundays Only'. The next day ticket sales doubled.

# AUTHORITY

Every society has authorities that help it function. We have teachers, law givers and law enforcers. We have leaders and managers. Every society and sub-group functions by virtue of having a social order. Every society has symbols of authority. We become accustomed to taking our lead from people in authority. Our brains create a short-cut. Very often, we don't ask questions, we just respond automatically to the signs and symbols of authority. If you have certificates or a white coat or a title, people will tend to believe what you say. They will even give a higher estimate of someone's height if that person is introduced with a title. My producer noticed that after half an hour on stage I look taller.

Authority does not come from having a loud voice, it comes from signs and indicators. Official stamps, uniforms, warning notices, formal titles, documentation and ritual introductions are all used to establish authority. When a judge enters a court, everyone in the court is asked to stand up. After the judge sits down, everyone else sits down. This little ritual doesn't make justice more just, but it reinforces the authority of the judge.

In America money is a sign of status and power and hence authority. When I first moved to Los Angeles I wanted to buy myself a vintage Rolls Royce Corniche. As a kid, I had watched the movie *Ten* in which Dudley Moore drove around Hollywood in a Corniche, and now that I had made it to LA

I wanted to do the same.

My manager said, 'You can't do that.'

'I can,' I said. 'I can afford any car I want!'

'No,' she said. 'It is not about what you can afford. You can't drive an old car in Hollywood. People will think you are poor. You have to buy a new one.'

My first thought was, That's ridiculous, but actually she was right.

Hollywood is a ridiculously competitive business environment, and the convention is that successful people all drive new, expensive cars. Of course, I could drive any car I wanted, but in Hollywood that is the equivalent of going to a business meeting dressed in a ripped sweatshirt and dirty jeans. It was simpler just to play the game.

Automatic respect for motor cars is not confined to Hollywood. In one study done in San Francisco, it was found that motorists would wait significantly longer before sounding their horns at a luxury car stopped at a green traffic light than an economy model.

The same rules, with different signifiers, apply in the City of London. If you are serious about a career in the city you go to work in a good suit with a smart tie. You can turn up in other clothes but you would be expected to have a good reason for doing so. These conventions have some significance. In Hollywood a new expensive car is an indicator that you do have at least enough money to run it. In the City of London a good suit shows you respect the conventions and are similar to other financiers and hence implies that you are likeable and trustworthy.

The human tendency to use automatic thinking and assumptions means that people react to symbols of authority without assessing whether they are well founded or even relevant. Hence the mere appearance of authority is influential.

That business suit can even have an effect outside the office. Some social psychologists asked a colleague to cross a road when it was reasonably safe but the signalling indicated *Don't walk*. Half the time he was casually dressed, half the time he was wearing a suit. He was followed by significantly more pedestrians when he was wearing a suit.

You don't need an expensive car. You don't need an expensive suit. Sometimes just a card will do. If you hire a jet-ski in Italy you have to get a little pass to wear that shows you are allowed to drive it. At the end of a holiday I arrived at the airport to discover no queues at all, just a total scrum at check-in. I took the pass from around my neck, held it up in the air and moved forward saying, '*Scusi, scusi.*' The crowd parted like the Red Sea and I made my way directly to the check-in counter.

When you encounter any of the symbols of authority – titles, uniforms, degrees and displays of wealth – remember these are just symbols. The two questions to ask yourself are:

1. **Is this authority real?**
2. **Is this authority relevant?**

## Using authority

Authority is the simplest tool of influence. With authority when you ask for something, it happens. Most of the time if you are confident, courteous and optimistic and your request is reasonable, then you will get what you want just by asking. In situations of confusion or danger, people will follow the first man or woman to lead with confidence.

One important distinction will help you to make the best use of your authority. Use authority to achieve a specific goal. Do not use authority to claim or attempt to achieve more status. Authority is already a form of status. Someone trying to use it to get more status lays themselves open to ridicule. Every so often you read of a celebrity somewhere losing their rag and shouting, 'Do you know who I am?' If the other person doesn't know or, as is more often the case, believes it is not relevant, then shouting about it won't help. It just reduces their authority.

Asking for what you want and confident leadership are both behavioural signs of authority. If you behave with authority, you don't need symbols. Nevertheless, as in Hollywood, you can make life easier by showing people the symbols they want to see. That's why doctors and dentists have their qualifications hanging in a frame on the wall of their reception areas.

All the preparation in Chapter 2 will help you build your natural authority, and the more you use it, the more natural it feels to you, and hence the more powerful its effect.

## ASSOCIATION

Perhaps the simplest and yet most persuasive form of influence is association. If I want you to like something, I put it next to something you already like or I ask a person you like to recommend it. We see association used over and over again by the advertising industry. Celebrities endorse products and sales to their fans increase.

Adverts of all kinds use good-looking models because research demonstrates that we are more attracted to people we rate as good-looking, and when we are drawn to them we are also drawn to the products in the advertisement. That's why you see good-looking women in adverts for almost anything, from ball-point pens to double-glazing fittings.

What is more, some of the attractiveness of the models seems to transfer to the product. A study in the 1960s showed some men a car. In one group the car was seen in a picture including an attractive woman. In the other group the picture did not include the woman. The men who saw the attractive woman rated the car as faster and better designed than those who saw the car alone. The presence of the woman changed the assessment of the car, yet when questioned afterwards the men denied that the presence of the woman had any effect on their rating.

Modern advertisements are generally more sophisticated, but the power of arousing positive emotions and associating them to your product is so strong it can still be used effectively with no rational or logical support whatsoever. I recently saw an advert that featured a chef talking about cheese. I'm guessing the chef was well known, if not well known to me. His script was basically this: 'Cheese tastes great. It's a good feeling eating good cheese. Bank XYZ makes you feel good too.' Cheese has nothing to do with banking. But the ad made cheese-lovers feel good and then associated 'Bank XYZ' with that feeling.

With streaming and online viewing, fewer people see the traditional ad breaks of broadcast TV. So advertisers now pay to place their brands inside attractive movies and serials. This is product placement. Often there is no promotional language, just a shot that includes the brand. The motor of association still works.

People selling houses are advised to roast coffee beans and put flowers on the table. The smell of the coffee beans and the beauty of the flowers don't change the actual house at all. But both the flowers and the smell of coffee are pleasant and the pleasure gets associated with the house and enhances its attractiveness.

Association is such a widespread motor of influence that it is impossible to sum it up. It is frequently used alongside social proof. I bought a suit the other day from a good, but not famous, brand. In a short conversation the salesman mentioned that the style I was looking at was very popular (social proof), it was frequently mistaken for a much more expensive brand (association) and a similar suit had been worn by a celebrity to the Oscars (association and authority).

## How to use association

You can harness the power of association with a technique called 'anchoring'. Perhaps one of the world's most famous experiments demonstrated the strength of association, and it was also a wonderful example of what we now call anchoring.

Russian scientist Ivan Pavlov rang a bell every time he fed his dogs. The dogs soon associated the sound of the bell with food so they would salivate. Very soon he could induce the dogs to salivate simply by ringing the bell. Pavlov had anchored the salivation response to the sound of the bell.

At my seminars I teach people how to anchor particular emotional states to the physical feeling of pressing together a finger and thumb. The attendees vividly remember an occasion with a powerful positive emotion, such as the first kiss of a new relationship, the moment of winning a race or the moment of stepping in to a new home. They remember the incident with such sensory vividness that they feel the positive emotion all over again. At that point I ask them to press together a particular finger and thumb. They do this procedure several times, thus creating an association between the feeling in their finger and thumb and their internal emotional state.

After several repetitions attendees are able to re-experience that positive emotional state simply by pressing together their finger and thumb. This is called creating an anchor.

You can create anchors linking all sorts of different

thoughts and emotions with all sorts of different sensory cues.

You can create anchors for yourself and you can influence other people by creating anchors for them. When I first learned about anchoring I had a girlfriend who didn't really like curry. For a few days, whenever she was hungry I touched her on the same point on her shoulder and said something like, 'Yes, you are so hungry you could eat anything, right?' Then one evening I touched her in exactly the same place and said, 'Do you fancy a curry?' She agreed!

When you start creating and using anchors you realize they are all around us all day long. We are all surrounded by advertisements that are busy creating associations between products and good feelings and anchoring those feelings to their brand logos.

## ANCHORING

*This exercise makes an anchor to activate your confidence.*

1. Think of a time you felt confident and energetic.

2. Remember the occasion as if you are seeing it now through your own eyes. See what you saw, hear what you heard and feel what you felt.

3. Make the colours brighter, the picture sharper and the sounds clearer.

4. Make the experience more and more intense until you feel in yourself now the same emotions of confidence and energy that you felt in this experience.

5. Now press together a finger and thumb. Match the pressure of your finger and thumb to the intensity of your feeling.

6. As soon as the intensity of the memory or feeling begins to fade, let the pressure and the memory go.

7. Look around and do something else for 2 or 3 minutes.

8. Next, repeat steps 1 to 7.

9. Do this 3 times. Wait 5 minutes. Then press together that finger and thumb and notice the feeling coming back and the memory reviving.

10. If necessary, repeat the exercise 3 times a day until you elicit a strong feeling of confidence and energy whenever you press together that finger and thumb.

## Sophisticated communication

The more you practise using anchors and spotting associations, the more creative you will become, and you will start using them in your own way. I just want to tell you now about one more technique that is particularly useful if you want to guide someone away from one behaviour and towards another. I use this in therapy and I also use it when I am giving a talk or pitching an idea. In the Western world people read from left to right so if you look at a painting or a theatrical stage there is a general tendency for movement towards the future to be movement towards the right. It is not always true, but most people most of the time will subconsciously associate things presented to their left with the past and things presented to their right with the future.

So when I am talking to someone I want them to put bad things in the past and associate the good things I am presenting, selling or explaining with the future. I can do this very simply by what is called 'spatial marking'.

If I am facing them I just make gestures with my right hand (which is to their left) when I talk about problems or difficulties or undesirable elements, and when I talk about stuff I want them to like and move towards I make a gesture with my left hand, which is on their right. I want them to move away from bad experiences, leaving them in the past, and move towards the good things they are buying, learning or receiving from me, putting them into their future. If the other person talks about something else they really like, I can link that to my spatial marking by gesturing with my left hand as I agree, thus linking their good feelings and my proposition.

# RECIPROCITY

I had a friend staying from out of town recently. She came back from shopping with a small piece of soap and two very expensive jars of skin-care treatments. She explained how someone had given her the soap and then explained the virtues of the skin-care treatment. She had been offered a special deal of a package worth over $500 for a mere $350 but decided instead to spend only $250. That still sounded like plenty of money to me, especially as she had not been looking for any skin treatments when she set out in the morning. What had persuaded her to spend so much? A small piece of soap, smaller than the complementary bar you find in hotel rooms. And how was the soap so persuasive? Because it was a gift.

When we accept a gift it creates a feeling of wanting to give something back. People hate to feel indebted so they have a strong urge to give something back in order to get rid of the feeling of indebtedness. Psychologists call this reciprocity. Reciprocity helps societies grow and function efficiently because we can do favours for others knowing that they will experience a strong pressure to do favours for us in return. Anthropologists have found evidence of reciprocity in both historical and contemporary societies all over the world.

Because reciprocity is an automated human response, it is an excellent way to influence people. For example, an Indian supermarket invited customers to cut themselves a slice of cheese as a free sample and sold an amazing one thousand pounds of cheese in just a few hours.

Reciprocity is a very powerful tool of influence because the feeling is not proportionate to the gift. You can give a tiny gift – a small piece of soap, for example – and cause the recipient to feel indebted to you and, importantly, they may not even realize it. In the experimental context, social psychologists have demonstrated that a small act of kindness, like giving someone a soft drink or a cup of tea, can influence them to spend significantly more money when you later ask them to buy raffle tickets for a charity. The free sample, like my friend's tiny bar of soap, is a popular and effective means of increasing sales.

You can use reciprocity to influence people by doing them a small favour before making a request of them. If you have just bought them a coffee, given them some information or even just lent them a book, they are more likely to agree to your request.

The habit of reciprocity is so embedded in us that sometimes in negotiation one party offers a concession in the expectation that the other party will do so in return. If that party is you, you don't have to offer a concession yourself. You could offer to buy lunch instead.

The most powerful defence against reciprocity is being aware of it. Whenever you notice that you are feeling obliged to give something or buy something or do something, review what has just happened and ask yourself, what triggered this reciprocity feeling? Then ask yourself, do I actually want to act on this feeling, and if so, in what way? Sometimes a sincere and heartfelt 'Thank you' is enough to make the feeling go away.

If you want to use reciprocity to influence others, remember that the strength of the feeling is independent of the value of the gift. A small, genuine act of generosity is enough to trigger it. A very successful trader in the City of London was walking back from lunch with his brother and passed a BMW showroom. His brother stopped to admire one of the gleaming motors.

'I'll get you that,' said the trader.

'No, no, no,' said his brother, 'that's crazy. It's really expensive.'

'Don't worry about it,' said the trader. 'You bought lunch.'

Practise reciprocity with your own random acts of kindness. Paying compliments and other small acts of politeness will generate goodwill all around you through the power of reciprocity. You will make the world a better place and you will find the world is kinder to you. Your generosity does not have to be lavish, but make a specific note to be kind, helpful and generous to people whom you wish to influence.

## Getting agreement

Have you noticed that when you are on holiday, the shop assistants often ask questions like, 'Are you visiting from out of town?' or 'Are you on holiday?' They aren't really looking for information. The reason they ask is precisely because they already know that the answer is yes. They are manoeuvring you into a state where you are agreeing with them. If you have said yes to their question you are more likely to say yes again and to make a purchase in their shop.

When I was learning about hypnosis I came across the same pattern in hypnotherapy. Therapists call this 'building a yes set'.

The remarkable American psychiatrist and hypnotist Milton Erickson used to say to his clients, 'Please could you close the door, and perhaps move the chair a little closer and sit down, and now can you notice your breathing deepen and when you are ready go into a trance?' It is very likely that the client will want to agree to each of these questions. They don't need to say anything, they can just respond by nodding and in responding to the fourth question they can notice their breathing deepen. Erickson has built a state of agreement in the client and will continue by building on this to induce a trance.

There are endless ways to vary this theme. For example, I might say to a client, 'You have come here today for a reason and listening to me now you have already had thoughts about this process and as you become more comfortable you may not know exactly when you go into trance.'

The yes set is one of the oldest sales techniques. I was in a store the other day and an assistant said to me, 'I noticed you looked at the coats and then you looked at the jackets. Maybe you will find these of interest?' As he mentioned what I had already done, at a subconscious level I was agreeing with him, and hence more likely to look at what he was showing me. I didn't buy anything but I noticed his simple use of the yes set.

The same pattern can be used in almost any sales environment. For example, 'You want value for money and you want someone you can trust.' Then, with a light gesture to yourself, 'Maybe I can help you?'

A yes set has no inherent logic. If we take up a certain attitude or feeling, it tends to carry on. People are more likely to agree to a request if they have said yes to one or two other questions beforehand. It is as though there is a psychological form of momentum.

It won't continue indefinitely. If you ask fifty questions to which the answer is yes, people will begin to vary their replies just because they get bored. Experience shows that one or two questions are a good set-up for assent to the third.

Sometimes we don't even have to ask a question to build a yes set. We just need to make a true statement which someone is likely to agree with. You have decided that today is a good day to learn more about influence, and as you carry on reading I'd like you to make a firm commitment to practising all the exercises in this book. If you agree with someone it highlights that you have something in common, so it also contributes to building rapport.

# CONSISTENCY

One extraordinarily powerful form of momentum is associated with our self-image. Human beings like to appear consistent. We really like it. We particularly like to be consistent about something we feel proud of. When we assert a position, the more effort we make and the more public the assertion, the more strongly motivated we are to stick to it. Hence, although we like to think otherwise, we have a tendency to be the opposite of open-minded. The more we assert something, the less open-minded we become.

If people have invested heavily in a certain opinion they may continue to assert it even in the face of clear evidence to the contrary. If the statement is written down we are even more inclined to stick to it. We are likely to use our intellect and our energy to defend our positions rather than to examine them critically. This tendency is the basis for some of the most powerful and extraordinary examples of influence.

Psychologists describe this in many ways, for example, as attachment or pride or ego-driven behaviour. The key point is to note that this human tendency makes us vulnerable. If we express an opinion or make a commitment it will influence our own future behaviour.

Advertisers, manufacturers and retailers know about consistency. Robert Cialdini cites a neat use of the principle by a toy manufacturer to boost their post-Christmas sales slump. The manufacturers extensively advertised their product before

Christmas to ensure that many children asked their parents for it as a present. Then they deliberately undersupplied the product to the stores so that lots of parents were unable to get it for their children and had to buy something else instead. However, the parents, not wanting to let their children down and wanting to be good parents, went back after Christmas and purchased the original product in order to stay true to their word, to stay consistent with their commitment. The manufacturers used consistency to make the parents buy twice as many toys as they originally intended.

There are also some less tricksy uses for consistency. I frequently ask my readers to write down their goals because research has shown that we are more likely to follow through on commitments that we make in writing.

## Invisible power

A study conducted by Stephen Sherman shows what a subtle but powerful force consistency can be in the most mundane of settings. In a normal suburban setting, a caller asked residents as part of a survey how willing they would be to give three hours of their time to go collecting door to door for a popular charity. Many said they would. A few days later a different person called to ask if they would in fact volunteer to collect for the American Cancer Society. The consequence of the survey was a sevenfold increase in the number of volunteers.

By saying yes to the survey, respondents had portrayed themselves as generous volunteers. The force of consistency made them consent when they were asked for real. This event is neither dramatic nor particularly memorable, and that is all the more telling.

We are very often unaware of being influenced by consistency. For example, you might not think you are being influenced if a caller begins a phone call with, 'How are you doing today?' and you reply, 'I'm fine, thank you.' But in another study, cited by Cialdini, consumer researcher Daniel Howard raised commitment to a charitable activity from 18 per cent to 32 per cent simply by asking this polite, everyday question before asking for help.

Why did it make a difference? We can see several factors at work here. First the caller built a little rapport simply by expressing an interest in the respondent's health. Then they increased the rapport by creating a moment of conversation (an experimental variation revealed that the question evoked twice as much compliance as the bald statement 'I hope you are feeling well'). Third, by drawing attention to the respondent's happy state, the caller subtly sets up a consistency obligation. The request that followed was to help provide meals for the needy. To avoid the inconsistency of being in a happy state and being uncaring about the needs of others, respondents were more likely to agree to help. Note that the pressure was not overwhelming. Two-thirds of respondents still said no. But the number who did say yes was nearly doubled.

This is one of the reasons fund-raisers often ask people to sign petitions in the street. They may not expect the petition to have any effect on the company or government department to which it will eventually be presented. They do know, however, that it will have an effect on you if you sign it. It will make you more likely to donate to them and more likely to identify yourself as a supporter of their cause.

## The truth about brainwashing

A far more extreme example of the power of the consistency principle occurred during the Korean war in the 1950s. When the Chinese captured American servicemen, they used the principle of consistency to change their loyalties.

It was a big task reprogramming men who had been highly trained to give only their name, rank and serial number. It was done very slowly. During an interrogation prisoners were persuaded to make one or two mildly anti-American or pro-communist statements. (For example, 'The United States is not perfect' or 'In a communist country there is no unemployment'.) Once these apparently minor statements had been given, the prisoner would then be asked to define exactly how the United States was not perfect. After some time he would be asked to sign his name to the list of reasons. Later he might have to read his list in a discussion group with other prisoners. He would be reading what he had said and signed himself.

The Chinese would then broadcast his name and list of reasons during an anti-American radio programme, not only to his camp but to all the other North Korean POW camps and the American Forces in South Korea as well. Suddenly he found he had become a collaborator.

When fellow prisoners asked why he had done it, he couldn't claim he had been tortured. He had to justify his actions, he had to stay consistent with his public commitments in order to confirm his own internal sense of identity. Therefore he would have to say that what he said was true. In that moment his self-image changed. He now believed he was pro-communist and his fellow prisoners reinforced his new identity by treating him differently. Before long his new commitment would make him collaborate even more with the Chinese to maintain the consistency of his new self-image.

## Using consistency

Consistency will be effective when your subject identifies with the cause or characteristics you are promoting. If we own an attitude or a belief, we make it part of our self-image. We like to have a consistent notion of ourselves, so once we have identified with a cause or attitude we tend to stick to it and defend it, because it feels like defending ourselves.

If we have expended a great deal of effort to get something we will value it more than if it was easy. Cults and secret societies have initiation rites which are painful or gruelling precisely because it makes the initiates value their membership all the more.

You can use consistency by inviting people to make a small statement or gesture in the direction of the outcome you desire. For example, if you are trying to mediate in a disagreement you might start by saying, 'I expect that we all would like this problem to be cleared up.'

If you are selling something, if you can get your customer to agree that they want to buy in principle, you are more than halfway to a sale.

You can defend yourself against being influenced by consistency very simply. You just have to learn to recognize it and be willing to say, if necessary, 'I'm sorry, I have changed my mind.'

# IN A NUTSHELL

- People run on habits most of the time

- People tend to follow the crowd

- People will respond to the appearance of authority

- Association and reciprocity influence us subconsciously

# NEXT STEPS

➤ Make a note of examples of social proof, scarcity, authority, association, reciprocity and consistency

➤ Reinforce your anchor for confidence

➤ Practise creating and using yes sets

➤ Practise spatial marking

➤ Perform small acts of kindness for people you wish to influence

# 5

·

# THE POWER
# OF PERSPECTIVE

## The power of perspective

The more information you gather about what is already happening, the easier it is to influence the people around you. Everyone you want to influence already has a history of beliefs, experience and desires. You never start from scratch, you are always joining in. That is why the most influential people I know, although very different in many ways, share two vital characteristics: they are very observant and very good listeners.

I have made plenty of mistakes in my time by making assumptions and sounding off before I had taken the time to listen. I have gradually learned the truth of the old saying that time spent in reconnaissance is seldom wasted. In fact, the more urgent the situation, the more valuable the information gathering.

I hold the belief that everyone has a story or something about them that is interesting. I want to know what it is. It is very rarely their views on politics or current affairs. It is very rarely who they know, or how much they know, or how clever they are. I want to know what they care about and why they care about it. I want to know their hopes and heart's desire.

If I meet a group of people, I observe how they interact. I notice who is organized, who pays attention to detail, who is most creative. I look for patterns of behaviour and indicators of status. I notice the person whom people are already following. The more knowledge I have, the easier my job.

## Gathering information

Gathering information is not a complicated process. It just takes curiosity, patience, persistence and politeness. When I start a therapy session I ask a very important question:

**'What do you want?'**

And when I get an answer, I question it again. I ask, 'And what will that give you?' and then again, 'Why do you want that?' I keep asking questions until I uncover the core values that are driving their behaviour. For example, one time the first answer I heard was, 'I want to lose weight.'

The conversation then went something like this:

I asked, 'And what will that give you?'

'I'll feel good about myself.'

'What difference will that make?'

'I'll be able to wear pretty clothes.'

'And what will that give you?'

'I'll feel confident. I'll feel attractive. I'll enjoy going to parties.'

'And what will you get from feeling confident and attractive and going to parties?'

'Well, I'll make friends, maybe I'll meet someone . . .'

There are many reasons people want to lose weight, such as health, comfort and self-esteem. In this particular case I discovered that the client was shy, she didn't feel attractive and a major motivation for her to lose weight was to find a romantic relationship.

## You have already started

You have already started the information-gathering process by practising your rapport skills. You observe posture, physiology and listen to all the variables of their speech. As you listen to their language and metaphors, you also learn about their map of the world and their values.

So-called 'small talk' before getting down to business in a meeting doesn't have to be 'small' at all. It is a perfect opportunity to find out more about someone's values and interests as well as building rapport. The key is to focus on the other person. Don't waste time trying to impress them, or tell them about your own life. Find out what makes them tick.

This seems in many ways very much a matter of common sense and even politeness. However, I find when I am teaching seminars a good number of students make a mess of it. They are in too much of a hurry. As soon as they find some common ground they launch into their own agenda, and they miss the opportunity to learn more about the other person. It seems that many of us need to learn to be patient and methodical. When I first meet people I usually do not yet know which particular information is most valuable, so I just keep an open mind and keep listening.

## OBSERVATION EXERCISE 1

1. Next time you are on public transport pay attention to three people.

2. When you get off the bus or train or whatever, write down as much as you can about each person. Start with simple observations, for example:

   Hair colour

   Eye colour

   What they were wearing

   Were they wearing spectacles? What colour?

   Were they wearing a wedding ring?

3. Move on to more subtle observations:

   Were they right- or left-handed?

   What indicators did you notice of their emotional state?

   What did you see and how did you interpret it?

## The advantage of flexible thinking

If you are having a conversation there are at least three ways to see it. The first is from your own point of view, known as First Position. Next is from the other person's point of view, known as Second Position. Finally, there is the onlooker's point of view, known as Third Position. People who use all of these positions have more flexibility in their thinking. These positions are particularly useful when you are dealing with conflict situations.

When Mahatma Gandhi was negotiating with the British for the independence of India he used the first, second and third position viewpoints. He believed completely in his own vision of a free and independent state, but when he imagined stepping into the shoes of the British negotiator he realized that the British thought they were doing a good and necessary job and ruling a backward country. When he stepped into the third position he understood that the British needed to hear that Indian people could run the country fairly and efficiently. He also realized that the British believed that they were helping the country and needed to satisfy their sense of obligation and dignity.

If you are gathering information in a new conversation, take the time to place yourself in each of these positions. Gather enough information about the people to whom you are talking to enable you to imagine hearing what you say from their position. Then imagine stepping aside from your own view and concerns and those of the other, and look at both from the outside.

# Know what is really happening

When I am doing therapy, I am on a relentless quest to find out what will bring about the changes that are needed. I am alert for where my client's energy goes up or down and whenever my interest spikes I know there is something important. I'm asking questions to find out what their core values are.

If the client is avoiding talking about what really matters to them, my job is make them feel comfortable and safe enough to do that. Sometimes people avoid speaking from the heart because they don't believe anyone would like them if they revealed their true selves. Actually your true self is what is most wonderful about you. It is unique. You are the only person in the world with your history, your point of view and the chance to write your own story. Wherever you are, you are the person best placed to make your own story wonderful.

If someone is shy, or initially reluctant to tell you what they really think or feel, take more time to deepen your rapport. When they feel safe enough you will help them to reveal themselves and discover the power and potential of being true to themselves.

## OBSERVATION EXERCISE 1

*These questions will help you hone your listening skills, practise first, second and third positions and get to the core issues in a conversation.*

1.  Check that you are building rapport.

    Have you noticed the speed and pitch of their voice?

    Have you noticed whether they prefer visual, auditory or kinaesthetic words or metaphors?

2.  Check that you are using all three positions to understand the situation.

    **FIRST** Ask yourself, what matters most to me?

    **SECOND** Now step into the other person's shoes and find out what matters most to them. Look back at yourself and see what you notice.

    **THIRD** What does the situation look like without the effect of the other person's concerns or your concerns?

## Framing

A photographer decides what to include in the frame, what to leave out, which angle to choose, where to focus, how much light to let in and what depth of field to use. In the same way, each of us is framing our perception of the world according to different interests, values and criteria.

For example, I might say, 'The Coffee Workshop is a great café' because it has delicious coffee. You might say, 'It's a terrible place' because the chairs are uncomfortable. We are talking about the same place, but see it very differently because our frames are different. My priority is taste, yours is comfort.

Everything we see and say has a frame around it, just as a painting or a photograph has a frame. The meaning of the picture or photograph is determined by the frame. Reframing – changing the frame through which someone or something is perceived – is one of your most powerful tools of influence.

Let me give you a few examples.

A famous TV commercial showed a young man pushing over an elderly lady. It looked like a mugging or gratuitous violence. Then you saw the same clip from a different angle and you saw he was pushing her out of the path of a pile of falling bricks. He changes from villain to hero simply by changing the frame in which we see him.

A while ago I was talking to Russell Brand and asked him what he had coming up. 'I'm presenting the MTV awards,' he said. 'To be frank, it's a little daunting.' I asked him to imagine his whole life as a long line stretching across the room from one side to the other and asked him how big the awards ceremony looked on that line. 'It's no more than the thickness of a sheet of paper. It's just another event.' The MTV awards are a big deal because the public vote for them. But within the frame of his whole career Russell could also see them as 'just another event'.

A reframe can be just a title. Many governments, including Britain, used to have a Ministry of War. Now they are called a Ministry of Defence.

Even the most trivial things can be radically altered by changing the frame. Using the frame of the present moment I can see the rain spoiling my day because I can't sit and write in the garden. Using the frame of the whole week ahead I see the rain as good fortune because it waters the garden and makes it more green and beautiful.

When I was a DJ I went to work for a boss who loved sport. He would say things like 'You've got to focus on the goal, Paul. Go for the back of the net. Play hard, but play with a straight bat.' He framed everything with sports metaphors, and I found that I got on better with him and understood him better when I used sports metaphors too, so much so that in due course we became good friends.

Frames can reduce or enhance credibility. When I started working with the issue of weight loss I realized that I had very little credibility with people who were seriously overweight. They could see that I wasn't fat, so they couldn't believe I would really understand their issues. I expanded the frame by explaining that I come from an overweight family. In that context, my words were more credible.

Reframing is often a component in a joke, and it can completely change our understanding. There is a story of two of America's greatest novelists, Kurt Vonnegut and Joseph Heller, at a billionaire's party in the Hamptons. They are surrounded by beautiful models, champagne is being served and there are millions of dollars' worth of art on the wall. Vonnegut commented on their host's enormous wealth surrounding them. 'Yes,' said Heller, 'but I've got something he will never have. Enough.'

I was watching Richard Bandler work with a woman and he reframed a problem of many years' standing with a single sentence. She had been engaged nine times but had never married. 'Why not?' he asked. 'I don't want to be disappointed or have my heart broken,' she said. 'Think how disappointed you will be,' he replied, 'if you get to the end of your life and you have not achieved your heart's desire.' In that moment he changed her perspective. Her frame was perfection; Richard offered her the frame of mortality.

Richard has trained many sales trainers. He teaches professional sales people to identify the primary frames of their customers and then to explain the benefits of the product in those frames. So if a customer talks about caring for their family, a car salesmen could emphasis how the safety features of his cars will protect the family. Incidentally, Richard calls selling 'helping people engineer their way through decisions'. This reframe helps people move away from the old-fashioned ideas of high-pressure selling and move towards an understanding of sales as assistance.

## Reframing for negotiation

There are circumstances in which people are hostile. They have very, very different frames but they are suspicious and they are not interested in changing their frames to be helpful. In those cases we can reframe by looking for a much larger frame within which they already agree. When my friend Michael Breen has to mediate between warring parties he will start by mentioning what all the parties share.

'We have come here today for the same reasons. We all want to find a solution that is satisfactory. We all have different ideas and we may need to be very frank to ensure our positions are understood. We cannot assume that we will easily reach a good resolution.'

Michael knows that he will reach a resolution more quickly if he starts with a frame that everyone agrees with, even if what they are agreeing about is the existence of problems. The frame of agreement provides a basis for more agreements to follow, one at a time. After a while the participants will feel the momentum of agreement and they will become more willing to consider potential solutions.

## Everything can be reframed

We can't see without having a point of view from which we are seeing. In the same way we can't think or speak without a frame that makes sense of what we think and say. We can always change the meaning of what we think or say by changing the frame.

There are countless ways to reframe things, actions and ideas. When I am deciding which frame to use, I imagine I am a photographer or filmmaker and I ask myself: How do I shoot this so that it looks most attractive to the person I want to like it? It doesn't matter at all what I personally think about it, or what I personally think is important. What matters is how my client or customer sees it. When you do this, everything you find out in your observation and rapport building will be useful.

Everything we perceive is filtered through our beliefs and perspectives. They form the default frame for our understanding of life. A great deal of my time as a therapist is spent reframing to allow people to see a richer world, a better future and more opportunities.

A year or two ago I was in the queue for immigration and the man next to me said, 'I've been trying to get in touch with you for ages! I'm a poker player and I've lost my luck.' During the time we were in the queue together I was able to explain to him the research of Richard Wiseman and Dean Radin about how we can create and change our luck, which

I included in my book *The 3 Things That Will Change Your Destiny Today!* Lucky people see the world differently and act differently because they consistently frame the world in terms of abundance and opportunity. As we parted I reminded him, 'You can't be that unlucky, because you found yourself standing next to me.'

## Comparison

Every comparison is a reframe. Sometimes you don't know much about the people you need to influence. In those cases a simple way to create a positive reframe is to make a comparison. So, for example, if I was selling a motorcycle for $10,000, I might point out that the performance is equivalent to a car costing ten times as much.

But let's take a more subtle way of using comparison. Let's say I am fund-raising for a charity. I might call you and ask if you would like to pay $5,000 to sponsor a table. Perhaps you will be flattered that I think you can afford so much. If you decline, I might follow up and ask if perhaps you would like to buy some raffle tickets at $10. I might even point out that you could buy a book of five tickets for $50. Ten dollars, or even fifty dollars looks like a small amount compared to five thousand dollars. That is the magic of comparison.

Comparison is also why salesmen always sell you the big-ticket item first. If you are buying a suit and a shirt, they will always sell you the suit first. Then a shirt, however expensive, will feel cheaper. If you are buying a new car, they will sell you the car on the basis of the list price, before adding in the cost of the extras, which may be very costly but seem to be less significant because of the much larger cost of the car.

A simple method to defuse the power of comparison is to immediately make another comparison that favours your perspective. Practise responding to comparison with alternative comparisons of your own until you have made it an automatic habit that will defend you against unwanted influence.

## Facts and frames

The more you become aware of frames and reframes, the more you realize that every point of view, every idea, even every fact is accessed via a frame. There are no fixed meanings in life. When you feel bad you see sadness and trouble all around you. When you feel good you see happiness and wonderful opportunities.

Take even the simplest fact. In the room in which I am sitting there is a table. That's a fact. It's true. The frame of this factual description is one we often use without thinking about it, which I will call 'physically accurate description'. But that frame does not include all the possible information about this table. If I say, 'This is the table I bought in France with my girlfriend', the same table looks different. This is the table we bought for our first home together, this is the table we used to eat together and plan our wedding. Now it has an emotional meaning.

Factual descriptions and scientific descriptions are frames that exclude subjective points of view. However, every person lives inescapably right in the middle of a subjective point of view, so a scientific or factual view can never capture the richness of what one person feels. You can't put love under a microscope, yet it is one of the most important elements of our lives.

'Science' and 'pure facts' are just two more frames through which to perceive the world. Everything we say and everything we hear or see or read comes inside a frame. A key skill of influence is to choose your frames appropriately. By the same token, the key to defending yourself against unwanted influence is to get into the habit of identifying the frames within which things or ideas are presented to you, and then to examine the same thing with a different frame.

## REFRAMING

*At my seminars I ask participants to make two lists: one of good things in their life and one of bad things in their life. Then I ask them to write down three negatives about the good things and three positives about the bad things.*

*I would like you to do the same, right now.*

1. Write down three things about which you have a positive feeling right now.
2. Write down three things about which you have a negative feeling right now.
3. Now next to each thing on your positive list write three negatives about it.
4. Finally next to each thing on your negative list write three positives.

So, for example, if you wrote at the top of your positive list 'My children', you might write 1) sleepless nights when they were babies; 2) financial burden when they were growing up; 3) stress, anxiety and arguments when they were teenagers.

At the top of your negative list could be 'My boss' and the positives would be: 1) taught me to stand up for myself; 2) brought me closer to my partner; 3) prompted me to apply for promotion in a different department.

# IN A NUTSHELL

- Everything is already framed

- Everything can be reframed

# NEXT STEPS

➤ **Practise observation**

➤ **Practise reframing**

➤ **Practise alternative comparisons**

# 6

·

# OVERCOMING OBJECTIONS

## Overcoming objections

I frequently don't know what to do. Not knowing is a very free and creative state and I use it a lot. Then, when I have done enough not knowing and something needs to be done, I remember two statements. The first is, 'There are many ways of getting it right.' The second is a saying of Milton Erickson, 'Always use what the client brings.' In every situation of influence there are always already relationships and energy between people. Everything is a potential source of influence. Utilization makes the best use of the things, relationships and energy that are already present.

## Utilization

Michael Elkin is a very skilful family therapist. He tells a story from a time in his youth when he practised a great deal of karate. He had reached black belt and was confident he could handle pretty much anything that was thrown at him. When he was walking down the street he would mentally rehearse how to respond if any of the passers-by attacked him. He was on a subway train one evening and a large, drunken man got onboard clutching a bottle in a brown paper bag. He looked like trouble. Michael prepared himself to intervene just as soon as he started harassing any of the women on the train. He was just deciding how to take him out when a high-pitched voice sang out, 'Hey, mister, what you drinking?'

The drunk swung round to see a little old Japanese man smiling at him.

'I'm drinking bourbon,' snarled the drunk, lurching over towards him.

'Sit with me,' said the Japanese man, patting the seat next to him. 'I like to drink sake. I drink it with my wife. Do you drink with your wife?'

The drunk collapsed like a burst balloon.

'She's left me,' he wailed.

The Japanese man patted his arm and talked to him. As Michael observed later, the old man was the real karate master.

The Japanese gentleman utilized the alcohol to gain rapport and defuse the situation. He also demonstrated his remarkable skills as a listener. Not only did he listen to the drunk's tale of woe, but as soon as the drunk got on the train he sensed the distress beneath the drunken bravado. His intervention completely avoided confrontation and elegantly offered the drunk the opportunity to talk about his troubles.

## Unlikely material

With utilization you can be successfully influential with the most unlikely material. In one of Milton Erickson's famous early cases he saw a young woman who was so depressed that she was contemplating killing herself. She was convinced she was ugly and would never find a boyfriend because she had a noticeable gap between her two front teeth.

A well-intentioned, common-sense approach might draw attention to all the good things in her life and perhaps try to use comparison to show how the gap between her two front teeth was relatively unimportant. There are two flaws to this approach. First, someone somewhere has probably already tried it, and it has already failed. Second, the gap is the central focus of her concern. There was clearly a lot of emotional energy attached to it. Any attempt to divert attention without addressing that central concern is likely to fail. Some people might suggest dental work to close the gap, and indeed that might have an effect. But it doesn't address the reason why a relatively minor issue in her appearance was having such a major effect on her life.

Erickson's approach to therapy was unusual when he was working in the 1940s and 1950s. He didn't place much emphasis on insight or understanding. He preferred to get people to do things and have experiences that would bring about healthy changes in their behaviour and outlook.

In this case Erickson intervened very directly in the young woman's life. She had very little dress sense so he arranged for her to be helped to buy new and more fashionable clothes and to have a complete makeover.

However, the central element of the therapy utilized this gap between her front teeth. Erickson persuaded her to practise squirting water through the gap until she was accurate at ten paces. He had discovered that a young man tended to go to the water fountain while she was there and, guessing he was interested, Erickson instructed the girl to squirt water at him using the gap between her front teeth. She did so. The man chased her round the office and asked her out on a date. Her life was so improved she no longer considered suicide.

Erickson's strategy was unorthodox then, and would probably no longer be considered appropriate now. The key learning is that Erickson embraced and used a core element of the problem to bring about the solution. There is nothing therapeutic about a gap between the front teeth, nor about squirting water. But Erickson used the thing she was most worried about to be the means by which she got some welcome male attention.

## Resistance

Traditional hypnotists used to talk about a person's unwillingness or inability to go into trance as 'resistance'. When you understand utilization, resistance doesn't exist. It is just energy waiting to be used. A hypnotherapist friend of mine once worked with a depressed woman who was desperate to feel better, but was simultaneously terrified of trance. She kept begging to be hypnotized because she was convinced it would reduce her anxiety, but as soon as she began to relax she would have a jolt of fear filling her with frantic anxiety. My friend tried all the different hypnotic inductions he knew over many weeks but both he and the client grew increasingly frustrated and depressed. Then one day he remembered Erickson's words, 'Use what the client brings.'

So he tried again. 'I can tell you are scared,' he said. 'In fact, even now you are frightened of what may happen and even though you hope good things will happen you are frightened now, so frightened you are like a rabbit, paralysed in the headlights of an oncoming car, you are scared stiff, frozen still, unable to move, and as you are unable to go into trance normally, you will have to go in backwards . . .'

With a few more words and few more seconds he had induced a catalepsy, the hypnotic phenomenon in which the client is unable to move. Her eyes closed and at last she went deep into trance and relaxed. After weeks of wasting time trying conventional methods, he finally used the fear and the resistance that she brought to help her to go into trance.

## Instant adaptability

I use utilization all the time, and frequently in combination with other techniques of influence. For example, the technique of pace and lead is built on the platform of utilization. I was coaching a friend of mine who was about to pitch a new programme idea to a network. He had been through weeks of preliminary meetings and now he had the big one. He needed to sell the idea of the show to the TV network.

I played the part of the network producer. My friend outlined his idea, a neat concept which combined audience engagement, voting by viewers at home and series-long competitions.

I interrupted. 'I think we should see elephants in this.'

'No, no,' said my friend, 'this isn't a circus.'

'No!' I replied. 'Wrong! If the producer sees elephants the correct response is, "Yes, how do you see that working?"'

The task my friend faced at the meeting was getting sign-off for his idea. The details could be worked on and changed later. He needed to pace the interest of the producer and make use of it. Maybe there really was a place for elephants, maybe there wasn't. But even if there wasn't, that was the idea that carried energy, so his job was to pace the energy now, and steer it in the right direction later.

## Start with what you have

Occasionally I will see a client who is in a very difficult situation and feeling anxious and depressed. I will lean forward and say, very sincerely, 'Good!'

And after they have had time to absorb the shock I will continue, 'You are in a bad situation and you feel terrible. That is a healthy response to a bad situation. Your body is telling you it is time to change.'

Here, I am employing both utilization and reframing. First, I am using what they have brought me, the depression. I don't try to minimize it or change it. I just use it to create a little surprise. That will help me to introduce a new point of view and new motivation.

Second, I offer them a different frame. I suggest that depression is not so much a problem as a signal, and a useful, healthy signal too.

As you continue to work through this system you will see many real-life examples can be analysed in terms of several principles and techniques. Rapport, reframing and utilization are the basis of a great deal of influence.

In business meetings, as in therapy, I am often clear about what I want to achieve but I may have no idea how I will achieve it. If I want someone to be interested in a new project I first of all want to find out what they are already interested in. I am building rapport, which may segue into pace and lead. I am always alert for opportunities for utilization.

## The core principle of utilization

Utilization is not confined to karate masters and therapists. I tell these stories because they are memorable. You can see from them that utilization is not really a technique. It does not have a set format or protocol. It is rather a principle: 'Use what is present.' It is an approach to all sorts of conversations, people and situations which allows you to maximize your influence.

Erickson published four volumes of papers and was interviewed many times. He never offered a theory of hypnosis but he did tell hundreds of stories about therapy and hypnosis, and utilization was perhaps the central element of his approach.

Almost all methods of influence are variations on the theme of utilization. When you are wondering how to influence another person, look around and find what is already happening and ask yourself how it can be utilized. Rapport and pacing and leading are perfect set-ups for utilization.

If you are a manager, a salesman, a therapist or a parent you will have opportunities every day to employ utilization. I devised a little exercise for my seminar participants to help them build the skills of utilization.

## UTILIZATION EXERCISE

*Practise this with a friend.*

1.  Establish a context – at home, at a business meeting or in a showroom.

2.  Choose a goal – for example, settling an argument, agreeing a policy or meeting a sales target (e.g. selling TVs, or insurance or cars).

3.  Ask your friend to start talking about something completely irrelevant to your context and goal.

4.  Find a way to use what they are talking about to introduce and promote your goal.

The point of the exercise is neither to be realistic nor successful. It is just an opportunity to practice utilization, and often reframing as well. There is no need to be plausible or brilliant. Just make whatever connections and utilization you can. You are just training yourself so that you see more possibilities and opportunities in real life.

*If you cannot find a colleague to work with, you can do the same exercise on paper.*

1.  On 6 separate pieces of paper or card describe a context and a goal. For example:

    context: interview, goal: to be offered a job

    context: retail computer sales, goal: to sell a laptop

2.  On another set of at least 4 pieces of paper, write a random selection of hobbies. For example:

    fishing

    football

    bird-watching

    snooker

3.  Shuffle each set of papers separately and then take one piece from each set.

4.  Find a way to use talking about the hobby you have picked and move towards the goal.

It is absolutely fine if at first this seems ridiculous or stupid. It is just an exercise to do in private or with a friend. When you practise a lot, you will become much more skilful and flexible in real life.

## Solution focus

In the 1980s Steve de Shazer and his team ran an unusual family therapy centre in Milwaukee. People could drop in to the centre and if there was a therapist free they could have a session.

Many of their clients had chaotic lives and a whole heap of troubles. Many were so disorganized that it was pointless to set up long-term therapy. In fact, even showing up for two sessions in a row could not be guaranteed. De Shazer and his colleagues could have tried to get their clients to become more reliable. They didn't. Instead they redesigned their therapy. They realized they might only see a client for one session so they didn't waste time on taking a history. They focused immediately on what the clients needed: solutions. And so the phrase was coined: 'solution-focused therapy'.

Typically the therapists never even ask the client why they have come to therapy. Steve would often open his sessions with the question, 'Are there any times in the recent or distant past in which the problem you are worried about did not occur?' He looks for exceptions to the problem, not at the problem itself.

Over time they built up a repertoire of ideas and questions, all of which guide their clients towards solutions. They are very simple questions. In every case they draw the clients' attention to what they are doing successfully, and ask them to do it more. The following are all very useful questions:

If this problem disappeared overnight, what would be the first thing you noticed tomorrow morning that would let you know things had improved?

If we meet in six months' time and your problem has been resolved, what would you tell me had happened?

What would be the smallest step that you could take today in the direction of the solution?

Being solution-focused works. It is extremely influential. The Milwaukee team regularly conducted outcome surveys among their clients and satisfaction rates were very high indeed, even after just one session. The solution-focus approach has now spread all over the world and it has been integrated into many different fields, including cognitive behavioural therapy. For example, Finnish family therapist Ben Furman has created a wonderful question to use when a meeting has reached a deadlock. 'I quite understand,' he will say, 'that it is impossible to move towards a resolution at this meeting. But so that we do not waste our time, I would like to ask each of you the following question: if we were to have a meeting, say two or three weeks from now, who would have to be present at that meeting in order for us to begin to move towards a solution?'

The question accepts what is happening but moves the focus to a solution, in an easy and non-threatening way.

Solution-focused thinking is not complicated. When I first came across it I couldn't believe that something so simple would actually make a real, lasting difference to people's lives. It seemed implausible that people with terrible, profound, long-term problems could be genuinely helped by such simple procedures. I was tempted to offer them clever, complicated solutions to match their twisted and complicated problems.

But, of course, life isn't like that. Being happy isn't complicated. Being in a mess is complicated. Good solutions and good agreements are simple. Complexity is expensive to administer and creates more opportunities for mistakes and fraud. So the bias towards simplicity in solution-focused thinking is extremely functional.

Solution-focused thinking is a very permissive form of influence, and it is all the more powerful because it is so gentle. It is a practical development of optimism. It draws attention to whatever is helpful and progressive and offers encouragement and support for doing more of the same.

## Business and therapy

Solution-focused thinking has many, many applications outside therapy and complaints procedures. It is the tactic of choice in any situation where people are stuck in a discussion of problems. It can transform family problems, management challenges, team building and planning strategies.

I have a friend who was training to be a therapist at the same time as his brother was studying for an MBA. The brothers were surprised to discover how often they found the same content, sometimes with a different label, in the management syllabus and the therapy training. The two areas of greatest overlap were change management and solution-focused therapy.

Both disciplines focus clearly on the desired outcome, and identify the simplest means of reaching it.

## Separate problems from people

We saw, when we were exploring the issue of consistency, that we can influence people very strongly if we induce them to build a certain position or activity into their self-image. It follows that if we want to change problematic behaviour it will help to separate the person from the behaviour. Therapist Bill O'Hanlon used to ask his clients how they 'did' their problem. For example, if someone told him they were depressed, he would ask, 'How do you do depression?' And if they found the question difficult, he would give an example. 'If I do depression,' he would say, 'I get up late. I don't draw the curtains. I don't get dressed. I go to the kitchen in my pyjamas and get some junk food then I go back to the bedroom and read self-help books.'

By turning the label into an activity, he separated the problem from the identity of the person. They could talk about 'depression behaviour' rather than 'depressed people'.

In the same way in the business world it is always easier to solve problems by avoiding comments that make it sound like people are the problem and keeping the focus on actions that can be managed.

## Negotiate any remedy

Solution-focused thinking is especially useful when there is a problem and you want to use your influence to secure a remedy. However much grief the problem has caused you, the secret to fixing it is not to convince the other party of how upset you are, but rather to motivate them to resolve the issue. If you do feel like making a complaint, before you say anything, or phone, or write an email, ask yourself what would a solution to the issue look like to you? Make sure you have a clear picture of what you want in your mind.

Next, make sure you are talking to someone who is capable and authorized to deliver the solution you require.

A friend bought a new apartment. Just two months after he had moved in, he went away for a month. On his return he found a false ceiling had collapsed and rain had come in through an open window and damaged the floor. The developers repaired the ceiling but wanted to charge for repairing the floor as they claimed he had left the window open. He believed he had not. However, he didn't want an argument, he wanted a solution.

He pointed out that the ceiling and the window had both been checked to the same standard before he took ownership of the flat. Furthermore he had, to date, refrained from publicizing the problems. When he mentioned publicity the developers saw the benefit to themselves in keeping him happy as they still had other apartments to sell. The developers fixed his floor free of charge.

## The value of persistence

A friend of mine was knocked off his motorcycle. There were many witnesses and the other party was clearly in the wrong. Fortunately his injuries were not too severe but he had a broken bone and torn ligaments.

The insurers for the other party offered him a payment of $6000 to compensate for his injuries and cover the cost of any future operation that might be required. He rejected it. Just over a year later he accepted a payment of $22,000. The only tool of influence used was persistence. He just kept talking and refusing offers and going for medicals until they raised their offer to an acceptable level. Persistence earned him $16,000.

If I feel someone has been unhelpful or is being uncooperative, I use persistence in a very intense way. I talk the person through the problem that requires a solution, and I ask them to step into my shoes and see the issue from my point of view, and see all the difficulties it has created. Then I make clear what I need them to do. I make them think that I have come to the end, then I begin again. I take them through the problem all over again and then once more I make them think I am finally coming to an end, and then I do it again. When I get to the required solution they are pleased to cooperate just to get rid of me.

## USING SOLUTION FOCUS

*Solution-focused thinking uses questions to reframe issues and draw attention to successful events and positive possibilities. It is not a specific technique to practise, it is more an attitude. Therefore, I suggest you become familiar with the strategies and questions below so that whenever you come across a situation that is characterized as a problem, you can influence it to develop towards a solution.*

- **Find out what is leading towards the solution, and ask for more of it.**
- **If someone mentions a problem, ask about exceptions: the times when it isn't a problem or when it doesn't happen. Ask them what they are doing at that time that is contributing to the absence of the problem, and ask for more of it.**
- **Separate problems from people and pay close attention to the positive potential of people.**
- **If you hear generalized negative comments, ask people to itemize exceptions to the generalization.**
- **Pay attention to what people do successfully and encourage more of it.**
- **Ask solution-focused questions:**
  - If this problem disappeared overnight, what would be the first thing you noticed tomorrow morning that would let you know things had improved?

- If we meet in six months' time and your problem has been resolved, what would you tell me had happened?
- What would constitute the smallest identifiable action you could take now in the direction of a solution?

My friend Michael Neill has his own version of this, as follows. He asks, 'If you were able to solve this problem, how would you do it?' Often the client replies that they don't know and that is why they are talking to him, but Michael insists. He carries on, 'Yes, I know, but if you knew, if you could solve the problem, what would that be like?'

And if the client continues to object he still insists. He will even say, 'Just pretend' or 'Make it up', and sooner or later the client starts to answer and they always come up with more of the solution than they knew they had.

# IN A NUTSHELL

- There is no resistance, only energy

- All energy can be redirected

# NEXT STEPS

➤ Always use what the client brings

➤ Notice issues, but focus on solutions

➤ Practise solution-focused questioning

# 7
.
# THE MOST
# EFFECTIVE SALES
# SYSTEM IN
# THE WORLD

## The most effective sales system in the world

Selling is not just about money. If you want your friends to go out with you, you need to sell them your idea. If you are a mum, you need to sell the idea of going to bed to your kids. If you are dating, you are selling yourself as an attractive proposition. If you want to join a sports team, you are selling yourself as a good player. And, of course, if you are selling a car, a house or a bicycle you are being a sales person even if that is not your day job. One way or another, everybody is selling all day long.

Maybe you sell your time, your expertise or your labour. Maybe you work as a sales person, maybe you work for yourself. Until you retire, you are always selling something: labour, services, items or ideas.

## Misconceptions about selling

Unfortunately for some people 'selling' is a dirty word. I believe this arises from sales people who are still using old-fashioned, high-pressure sales techniques. There are unscrupulous individuals who just want to make a sale and don't care about anything else. They are willing to lie or cheat and they don't care for their customers' interests.

I would like to see those people go out of business and the best way to put them out of business is to win their customers by doing the job better. Honest selling will build you a good reputation and get you more customers. For me, a good sales person is helpful. You identify the customers' real needs and help to meet them.

For me, there are four principles of selling:

1. **Only sell what you believe in.**
2. **If you've got it, sell it.**
3. **If you haven't got it, send the customer somewhere they can get it.**
4. **Never sell someone something they don't want.**

There are lots of people and organizations who sell courses in being a better sales person. They can give the impression that selling is complex, difficult and highly technical. They also like to give the impression that if you don't buy their technique you are missing out on a 'once-in-a-lifetime' opportunity. I'm sure you recognize that claim now as a version of the 'scarcity' method of influence. Don't worry about it, another 'once-in-a-lifetime' opportunity will be along soon enough.

I believe selling is a sophisticated but essentially simple process, and the skills of influence and charisma that you are learning here will enhance your abilities massively, whatever it is you are selling.

## A story that changed my life

I was very fortunate to meet and become friendly with Anita Roddick. She totally changed retailing by bringing ethical trading to the high street. Single-handedly she put ethics on the agenda of all major retailers. She inspired thousands of women to go into business. She built a business empire worth hundreds of millions of pounds and gave hundreds of millions of pounds to charitable causes. Her insights were a hugely valuable contribution to my book *I Can Make You Rich.*

Anita said to me that she never sold anything. All she ever did was tell people stories. 'I tell people about the things I want to achieve,' she said, 'and they get excited.' Anita's own story of building her business was the perfect example of the power of genuine enthusiasm. She was genuinely excited about ethical trading and about ending testing cosmetics on animals. She was a small woman who had a huge impact. She told vivid stories and gave people a compelling future to move towards.

## The foundation of sales: belief

Before you set out to sell anything, you must believe that what you are selling is valuable. Whatever you are selling, find something about your product or service that you really believe in. Find what makes you enthusiastic and excited about it. Your belief in your product will be manifest in all your non-verbal communication so your enthusiasm for what you love will do a huge amount of work for you.

If you don't believe in what you are selling, it will show, to some people at least. It also makes selling harder work, because you have to keep convincing yourself as well as your customer. It is simple to sell stuff you love. You don't need to love every part and every detail, but if you don't love it, move on.

There are some people who can sell almost anything. They can sell insurance or vacuum cleaners, houses or holidays, cars or kitchens. How do they do it? They enjoy helping people and making them happy. So long as they know the product is useful or enjoyable, that is enough to unleash their enthusiasm. If you are selling insurance, it may seem boring, but if you know it helps people sleep easy at night you can feel good about selling them that benefit.

I have worked for advertising agencies, political parties, governments and commercial organizations. But whatever I do, I interrogate what I am being asked to help to sell. If I can see its value, I'll do the work. When I can't see the value or agree with the goals, I turn down the work.

## Low-balling

Old-school selling was full of dirty tricks and a classic is called 'low-balling'. Low-balling means getting an agreement to purchase on the basis of a low price, and then adding in more costs afterwards so that the final price paid is inflated to what the salesman originally intended. It is a nasty trick which uses the consistency influence principle against customers. If you feel the pressure of consistency, you just need to say, 'The price has changed, so I've changed my mind.' Alternatively you can employ consistency against the seller.

My friend Michael went to buy a car. He had $60,000. He found a car and asked the salesman to confirm that the price, the final drive-the-car-away price, was $60,000. Yes, yes, said the salesman. So they sat down to do the paperwork, and as he worked through it the salesman added sales tax and administration charges and all of a sudden the bottom line was $70,000. Michael stood up and walked out of the showroom. The salesman chased him down the road trying to explain the tax. Michael stopped and said, 'You lied to me. You said $60,000 was the final figure.'

Eventually the salesman agreed to remove all the extra costs and Michael agreed to buy the car for $60,000.

As a buyer you will still meet old-school salesmen who try to use these kinds of techniques, but you don't need to fall for them any more. And as a seller I would like you to know you don't have to use them. There are far better ways to sell and to generate genuine good will.

## The journey

Selling is the journey from meeting the customer to closing the sale. It is not an argument or confidence trick. It is just a journey. A sales person is someone who guides the customer along that journey. There are many different routes to choose from which lead to the same destination. Sometimes the journey is very short, sometimes quite long. We will look at the typical stages of selling, but each journey is unique, so you won't pass through all of these stages each time.

## What makes people buy

People can use logic and are capable of being rational. This has caused a huge misunderstanding about how people actually make decisions. People can argue with logic, they can explain with logic, they can explore with logic, but ninety-nine times out of a hundred they make buying decisions based on emotions. When you want to sell to people, the very last thing you should think of using is logic. You need to change how they feel.

**People make decisions to buy based on emotion, not logic.**

The buying journey is an emotional journey. You start wherever the customer is and you move through different emotions until you reach a place of compelling motivation where the customer feels that the best thing to do with their money right now is to purchase what you are selling. That place is a specific internal, emotional state.

It may be that the customer talks about reasons for purchase, and you can talk about reasons too, if the customer likes that, but don't be distracted by rationality. Buying is an emotional decision. Research shows that the best time to sell to someone is immediately after they have bought something, because they are still in a buying state. My brother's very first job was working in a shoe shop. He was their best salesman by a mile. He used to sell a pair of shoes and he would make a point of admiring them as he packed them up for the customer. 'They look great,' he would say. 'You know, if you buy this brush and this polish you can keep them looking as good as new for years.' As customers had just agreed to buy, they found it easy to buy a little more. He was also using the influence technique of comparison as the polish appeared cheap by comparison with the shoes.

Everyone of us has had the experience of buying. If you think back, you will realize that even if occasionally many reasons were involved, sooner or later you had to make a decision – and the way you do it is emotional. You decided what you wanted. Even if you wrote out a list of pros and cons for an important purchase, the value you placed on each item in the pro column and each item in the con column was determined by your feelings.

So, remember, people make decisions to buy based on emotion, not logic.

## First, get their attention

The sales journey starts when you catch the customer's attention. We live in a world crowded with messages. Everyone wants our attention and our money, so when you are selling you need to make your message as clear and punchy as you can. A friend of mine asked me to see a young entrepreneur who had been selected to appear on a TV programme because he lacked a bit of confidence. I asked him to tell me about his business idea.

He intended to sell bags made of hemp to large retailers. The bags were eco-friendly, could carry advertising and would reduce the use of plastic bags. He told me about the factors involved in production costs in China versus India, about the manufacturing process and how the hemp is grown. I interrupted him and asked, 'What is the essence of your offer?'

'This will revolutionize shopping,' he said.

'That's it,' I said. 'That is your opener. That will catch their attention. The first thing to do is make sure they are listening. You can tell them all the other stuff later.'

Another friend worked with a truly excellent salesman called Frank. One day Frank leaped out of his chair waving a letter and saying, 'Yes, yes, yes!'

'What's going on, Frank?' asked my friend.

'I've got them,' replied Frank. 'Look,' and he gave him the letter to read. It was a polite letter rejecting Frank's offer.

'I don't get it,' said my friend. 'They're telling you to get lost.'

'Yes,' said Frank, 'but now they are talking to me! Before they weren't even answering my letters.'

Frank had caught their attention. The other party had entered into conversation and Frank worked on it until eventually he closed a deal.

Another attention-grabbing gambit is the free sample. If you play it right you will get two benefits. First, people will pay attention to something for nothing. Second, you will trigger the reciprocity response and your potential customer will have an unconscious pressure to respond to your free gift by giving some benefit to you in return such as, for example, making a purchase.

## Now build rapport

You've caught their attention, so now you hold it by building rapport. Rapport is not just about being liked and trusted, it also creates a clearer channel of communication. As you get on better, you can understand each other better.

This is why it is important to have a genuine belief in the

service or product you are selling. As soon as you are in rapport, you influence the other person, and if your words and your non-verbal communication are congruent, the other person will trust what you say. If you say you believe in something but your non-verbal communication shows you don't, people will pick up on the incongruity and they will assess you as less trustworthy, even if they are not quite sure why.

We saw earlier how to build rapport with individuals face to face. You can also do it with groups or sections of the public. We tend to like people who are like us, so many advertisements use models who are attractive in a 'girl-next-door' or 'guy-next-door' way. You might think that super-beautiful people would make the product more attractive but in most cases that is not true, because people identify with more normal-looking models in adverts, albeit at the handsome end of the normal spectrum. However, adverts do use very beautiful models to sell beauty products to imply that you too will look that good with this lotion, potion or mascara.

I have found that when some people first practise building rapport they are so excited they try too hard and do too much, particularly in a sales context. I find it useful to remind everyone that on the whole people want to be liked and want to be friendly. Often you don't have to do much. You can be relaxed about it, and your relaxation will put people at ease as well. Often all that is needed is a friendly 'hello' and building rapport is super-easy.

## Understand values

While you are talking to your potential buyer and building rapport, you are gathering information and discovering their values. Advertising agencies do this through market research before they launch a campaign. You can do it just by chatting and being interested. Find out what your customer likes and what they like to do. They will enjoy talking about it, their passion will make them interesting to you and it will reveal to you some of their values. Some people care most about aesthetics, some about practicality, some about status. If you are selling watches, you can help your customer find the right watch. Some people want a Rolex because it is a symbol of wealth and status, others want an obscure brand because they love the aesthetics of the mechanism, and some just want to look at their wrist and know what the time is.

By showing a genuine interest in people you set up many factors in your favour: you build rapport, you gather information, and triggering their passion and interest in the context in which you are selling puts the power of association on your side.

You will use the knowledge you gain about their values in the next stage.

# The most important thing I can tell you

These are the three most important words about selling:

**Sell the benefits.**

A car will transport you from A to B. That is a benefit. But it is only one of many, many benefits. A car can be a beautiful object. It can be fun to drive. A car is an environment in which to listen to music, to be comfortable and insulated from the world around. A car can deliver an intense, exciting driving experience. Others are as effortless as possible. The benefits of a car can be comfort, safety, speed, driving pleasure, relaxation, status, investment potential, robustness, ease of maintenance and so on and so on.

When you know the values of your customer, you know which of the benefits will be most important to them. To a man with young children, the most important benefits of the car will be space for children with all their clobber and the safety features that will protect his family.

To a golfer the most important benefit could be the fact that the boot is large enough for two sets of golf clubs. To a nightclub owner the benefit may be the coolness of the brand. To a keen driver the main benefit will be the performance of the car. To a person buying their first car the key benefit could be freedom from public transport.

I was discussing with Simon Cowell a new show I was

about to pitch to an American TV channel. I told him all about it. Simon said, 'This is too much information, Paul. Why should I watch this show? Tell me in a newspaper headline.'

'OK,' I said. 'Watch this show and you lose weight.'

That was it. That was the opening line of the pitch. The show was commissioned and it was a massive ratings success. The show had lots of other elements and benefits but Simon's question helped me to go straight to the unique, core benefit.

## SELL THE BENEFITS

*When you are selling, imagine the buyer is asking you the following five questions. The answers will clarify the benefits of your product or service.*

1. Why should I buy your product/service?
2. What do you have that is unique?
3. Why are you better than your competitors?
4. What will I get that I can't get elsewhere?
5. How does your product/service make my life better?

When you really understand how to sell the benefits, selling is simple. When I am teaching at influence seminars I find many people are hampered by the fact that they know too much about the history or manufacture of their products, or they have become used to telling their story in a certain way. I now ask people to practise selling the benefits of their business to each other as quickly and simply as possible.

I had one attendee who started by telling us that his company had existed for over twenty-five years. That was how he always started presentations about his company, but it is not a benefit. The benefit is trust or reliability. He finished by saying he believed his company was the best in its sector in the UK.

We turned his presentation around. He started by saying 'We are the best' and continued by listing all the benefits that supported his claim, which included trust, customer satisfaction, quality and reliability. The company sounded way more attractive and we had a better understanding of the benefits of doing business with him.

## What every sales person needs to know: inoculation

If you have an idea or a product to sell, people may have objections. Prepare to meet their objections by showing why they don't matter or showing how the benefits outweigh the objections. Very often it is better to bring up the objection before the other party does. You can use your explanation of the benefits to preempt their objections. Inoculation acknowledges objections but prevents them from stopping your sale.

For example, I was doing a training seminar on influence in Italy and I asked the participants what is the number-one objection they meet. As is common everywhere, the answer was price. I worked with one gentleman whose company sold air-conditioning. His units cost twice as much as the competition. He believed they were better than the competition but he was being outsold over and over again. I asked him to tell me more about his units. It turned out they were more expensive because he engineered them to last more than three times longer than his rivals and his units had almost ten times fewer technical problems. These were fantastic benefits but he wasn't really selling them and he wasn't overcoming the price objection. I suggested he build a rich sensory experience for his customers.

'Imagine it is a hot, sunny day. The cheap aircon breaks down and your staff are hot, sweaty and irritable. They can't concentrate, they are unhappy with their working conditions, their motivation declines and sales suffer. Just one rude phone call can screw up a million-dollar deal. An office full of complaining staff can ruin your reputation. It's not worth the risk. With aircon you can rely on, your staff will feel cool, calm and comfortable all day every day. With years of safe, efficient, reliable aircon, you have virtually no downtime, no irritation, no unexpected expenditure, happier staff, happier customers and a better bottom line.'

He needed to build a rich sensory experience of the benefits of his product, which reframed the cost within a picture of the whole lifetime of the product and thus inoculated against the objection of high price.

At one seminar a participant told me he was doing everything I suggested but he was still getting rejections. I am sure he was sincere, but it couldn't be right. However, I was not present at his meetings with his customers to see exactly what was happening. So I made the following suggestion. 'Go back to three of your customers who said no to you, people whom you feel comfortable with, and ask them why. Let them tell you why they said no. Their answers will show you what is missing and identify the areas you need to improve.'

If you meet objections to your idea, service or product, make a list of them all. Against each one write down the reframe or the benefits which overcome the objection and demonstrate the value of your proposition.

## The central secret of selling

Whatever you are selling, you are selling feelings. Richard Bandler trained the sales force of a company of home builders in a recession and they sold more homes than ever before. Richard taught them that, more than homes, they were selling feelings. They sold comfort. They sold value. They sold safety. They sold security. They sold convenience. They sold peace of mind. They sold lifestyle. They sold more homes in that year because they understand that all you sell are feelings.

If you are selling a big brand, you are selling the feeling that brand evokes in your customer. Coca-Cola is not just selling a drink. They spend millions on advertising which associates their drink with happy people, fun times and friendship. So when you buy a Coke you buy a bit of that feeling of friendship and fun times. Nike have the greatest sports stars in the world on their ads performing at their peak. Their fans associate good feelings with the stars, then the brand flashes up. It is so simple. It doesn't look like a hard sell at all, but it associates those good feelings with the brand and then the brand adds those feelings to their products. Nike don't just sell trainers. They sell that feeling as well.

Tell your customers about the feelings they will get when they own your product. Sometimes you can do this directly, for example, selling a house: 'Ask yourself, what would it be like to own this house?' Or you could say, 'Take your time to think about it. What would it be like to live here? Can you imagine how relaxing it will be to come home, have a drink in the garden and watch the sunset?'

## Meeting your customers' needs

If your product doesn't have what your customer needs, don't sell it to them. You will gain more long-term goodwill by directing him or her to where they can get what they need. If you manipulate your customer into buying what they don't want, you will generate buyer's remorse.

If you haven't got what they want, send them to the person who has got it. Everyone wins. That customer will become your best advertiser and will be influenced by reciprocity to repay the favour by sending people to you, and the person you sent them to will also be indebted and grateful to you.

Alternatively, when you don't have what your customers want, listen hard and build what they want. Porsche for many years have sold 911 sports cars to wealthy people. Some customers are older people who had several cars, but a good slice of their market is successful, young, single professionals.

Eventually those young singles grow up and have children, and pretty soon a 911 is an impractical car. Porsche realized they had loyal customers but no product for them. They liked the Porsche feel and the Porsche brand, but there wasn't a Porsche family car. So Porsche created the Porsche Cayenne. Porsche did not need to steal customers from Land Rover or Jeep. They created their Cayenne because they already knew there were customers for the benefits it delivered: Porsche values with practical space for a family.

When I was looking for a car in London I found a beautiful old Aston Martin, but the salesman said he wouldn't sell the car to me before I had driven it for the day. 'The clutch is heavy,' he said. 'It would make a great weekend car, but if it is your daily transport in London you need to be sure you can deal with it.' I drove the car and found he was right. The clutch was too heavy. I didn't buy the car, but I have recommended him to other people.

## Creating positive states

You will increase sales by generating positive states and linking them to yourself, your product or your service. Make your customers feel excited and happy. When you want someone to feel something, go there yourself first. Maintain rapport and you will lead your buyer to feel good about it too.

Because people make buying decisions based on emotions,

not logic, any good feeling you can associate with your offer will help to sell it. That's why being welcoming, polite and friendly is not only nicer but also leads to more sales. Almost all shop assistants are trained to say the right words, but it only works if they mean it. When you are genuinely friendly it makes all the difference.

Conversely, negative feelings can stop a sale instantly. Most of us have had the experience of deciding to leave a shop because the sales person was rude.

When you are selling a service, don't be shy. Use all the techniques from Chapter 2 to boost your internal state and enjoy meeting your customers. Smiling and paying compliments makes everyone happy when you really mean it, so find out what makes you happy about your job or service and share that feeling.

## What motivates people

We all like to feel good, but many of us find relentless positivity a turn-off. It may be that we can't believe anyone can be so happy 100 per cent of the time. It may be that sometimes people feel a bit low and need that feeling to be properly paced before it is time to let it go. Or it might be the sort of realism that says life is not a permanent high and it is sensible to acknowledge that life is sometimes painful or difficult.

If you feel there is a need to balance all the good feelings, it can help to mention problems, but you can still make them work for you. You don't just show people benefits and good feelings to move towards. You also show people problems or difficulties from which they can move away.

One of my hypnotherapy students enjoyed helping people give up smoking. Before using hypnosis he would briefly explain that they were not really giving something up. Rather, they were taking up a new, fresh, delicious, healthy lifestyle. Then he would pause and ask, 'Do you know how far it is from your home to the nearest cemetery?' He would tell them that every cigarette they smoked was leading them to an early grave. He would ask them to imagine a line of cigarettes, lying end to end, running from their living room all the way to the cemetery. Every cigarette they smoked took them one step closer to the cemetery. Alternatively, they could stop smoking. His set-up offered a vivid picture to move away from and a fresh, healthy lifestyle to move towards.

When you feel comfortable with spatial marking you can reinforce your words by anchoring all the problems to move away from in the past to their left, and all the positive feelings and your buyer's positive remarks, along with your product or service, to their right in the future.

If you recognize that your customer is a polarity responder you will often find it is easiest to begin by mentioning all the problems they have to overcome. Wait a while and don't mention how your services will solve them. More often than not you can watch your customer talk themselves into the sale.

## How to avoid errors

Occasionally I find that people have made their lives difficult by three common errors.

Error number one is for a seller to give the customer information that is not relevant to their needs. Don't bore your buyer with endless detail. Elicit the buyer's values and focus on them.

When I buy a phone, I want to know is it reliable, is it easy to use, is it good value? So if you are selling to me you need to find that out and find a phone that delivers that.

Another example is that market research has uncovered that more people make their final choice of a sound system based on what it looks like, rather than what it sounds like. If you are a hi-fi sales person you need to remember when to stop talking about the technical specifications. Let your customers talk about how good it looks.

Error number two is to use arguments to convince the buyer of the value of your services. You may believe that your insight should be significant to the buyer, but if it is not, it is not. Even if you believe that you are objectively right, it still doesn't matter. Your job is not to convince anybody of anything, but rather to use and respond to the values your buyer already has. What matters is your buyer's subjective opinion. Remember, buying decisions are emotional, so sell the benefits that the buyer appreciates and generate positive states.

Error number three is to create a counter-productive

association. Fifty years ago Imperial Tobacco launched what was widely regarded as one of the worst advertising campaigns of all time. They launched a new brand of cigarette called Strand with the tagline 'You are never alone with a Strand'. The TV commercial showed a man smoking all on his own. Even though the verbal message was notionally positive, the commercial created an association between loneliness and Strand cigarettes, so the public associated the brand with loners and losers. Sales were disastrous and the brand was withdrawn.

That story of failure is widely known, but just a few years ago I saw the same mistake when I was consulting at an ad agency. A sporting brand created a high-energy commercial for their new season and they didn't understand why it was testing badly. The final shot before the brand logo flashed up at the end was of a crunching, painful tackle. It was certainly an exciting sport, but it made the viewer wince just as they saw the logo. That was not a good association.

## The most important question for influencers

Over the years I have been through the process of creating a TV show many times and a critical moment in development is the pitch meeting with a channel or broadcaster. Before those meetings I ask myself the question:

**What does this person need to hear, see or feel to say yes?**

I work out the answer as best I can from the information I have gathered then I imagine stepping into their shoes and seeing me and the whole situation from their eyes. Then I ask the question again, 'What does this person need to hear to say yes?'

For example, in a recent meeting I realized one key executive needed reassurance and safety, yet also wanted to be seen as creative. And everyone wants to commission a show that gets high viewing figures. So I told her about the new show. It was different from previous shows, but has elements that are similar to very successful shows currently running. I had been a guest on another show and done a taster of what we planned and it had been the highest-rated part of that show. I was able to show her that I delivered far more than my nearest rivals. I delivered results, not just feel-good stories. Then I shut up. She then began to describe how she saw it developing, and I knew that we had a winner.

This question puts a focus on the feelings and benefits that you need to convey to your buyer. Sometimes it will highlight what is missing. It is always a great question to ask yourself before you close a sale.

Occasionally you may realize that you are not sure of the answer. In that case one potential solution is just to ask your buyer directly:

**What do you need to hear, see or feel to say yes?**

The answer they give is a direct route to making your sale.

## Reason to believe

We know that buying decisions are emotional, but many people like to feel that they are rational. They look for a reason to justify their decision even though it wasn't really why they made the decision in the first place. Marketeers call these 'supports' or 'reasons to believe'. Social proof, psychological momentum, authority and scarcity can all be used to create reasons to believe. Sometimes you can tell that someone is keen to buy but they are still looking for a reason to justify their decision. You may discover what they need from asking, 'What do they need to hear to say yes?' Alternatively, you will have a hint if you have noticed their preferred style of thinking. People with a visual bias may be looking for something concrete they can see. Show them a picture, or a contract, or, if you can afford to throw in a sweetener, show them what you can give them. People with an auditory bias may need to hear more about it. You can tell them that this model is popular (social proof), that it has very good reviews (authority), that it is selling fast (scarcity), or that it is a natural fit with everything they have told you (consistency). People with a kinaesthetic bias will respond to being able to experience the product through a test drive or a fitting or being given something physical like a free gift.

You never need to think about persuading anyone to buy things. Just think of your supports and reasons to believe as tools that help your customer to make up their own mind.

## The easy way to close a deal

The moment when a sale is agreed is known as 'closing'. As you integrate the patterns of influence into your conversation you will find that nine times out of ten your buyers will agree to purchase when you have sold the benefits and anchored good feelings to your product or service. Sometimes the buyer is ready to close before you were expecting them to. Be prepared. As soon as you've got a yes, stop talking. Many times I have seen people talk themselves out of a job or a deal or a sale because they missed the moment when the other party was ready to say yes.

If the other party needs a little help to say yes, you can build a yes set and offer some supports or reasons to believe.

I have been asked several times how to apply the right pressure to customers to close a deal. My reply is always the same, 'That's the wrong question.' Only poor salesmen apply pressure. Your goal should never be to apply pressure. Instead, you should always aim to build enthusiasm and excitement in the other party so that the impetus to buy comes from them.

When you sell a product you hand over the item. If you sell a service or agree a deal, always get a written document of the agreement. Even if there will be a full contract later, get both parties to sign a short heads of agreement at the time. Not only is it a record of the deal, but writing it down reinforces the commitment of all parties.

## What everybody needs to know about dating

Ever since I started working with hypnosis, people have asked me whether I have used hypnosis to seduce a woman. The answer is yes and no. I have never, ever, put a woman into a trance to get her to come to bed. On the other hand, I did become more persuasive when I learned about hypnotic language patterns. After all, when you learn the patterns of influence they become a natural part of your vocabulary.

When we flirt, we are selling ourselves to a potential partner. We are building a relationship, which means being authentic so they see who you are, and asking questions so you find out who they are. Don't try to impress people. Don't talk about your car, your marathon times or your place in the south of France. Ask questions. Get people to talk about themselves. If you feel the need to get in sync with someone, notice their preferred style of thinking. If they are visual, go to the movies. If they are auditory, go to a gig. If they are kinaesthetic, get active – play sport or go dancing.

The basic formula of flirting is very similar to sales. First of all, get their attention. Use your rapport skills and find out what is interesting about that person's character to you. If you are interest*ed*, you become interest*ing*. In conversation, use open questions. A closed question is one that can be answered with a yes or a no. An open question invites people to give you more information and allows the conversation to continue.

Second, once you have their attention, evoke positive feelings in the other person. Find out what makes them feel good and talk about it.

Third, when you make them feel good, anchor those feelings to yourself. You can anchor with a gesture, with a touch or just by catching their eye. It only takes a fraction of a second. The more you do it, the more they associate the good feelings with you.

This simple three-step model is the basis of Ross Jeffries' famous 'speed seduction' technique.

He would start with an open question to catch the attention and start a conversation, and follow up with: 'Have you ever been so in love with someone that you don't know what you are going to do next? I don't know if you, like me, were overwhelmed when you felt that,' then he would gesture to himself. Sometimes he would ask a woman if she had ever found herself unexpectedly aroused and again associate the memory to himself. This may all sound very mechanical, but this is what people who flirt successfully with each other do naturally every day.

Ross brought a lot of humour to the process and he demonstrates that we fall in love using our brain, but the key is the right brain, which is the seat of emotions and feelings, not the logical, calculating left brain. Personally I believe that if you really want to get to know someone, there is no need to be in a hurry. Take your time and enjoy the process.

It is said that women like men with a sense of humour. That may be true but I don't think that means we all have to be comedians. I think it means women like a man who makes them laugh and makes them feel good about themselves. It is also said that men go for good looks. That may be true, but being good-looking is more than genetics or cosmetics. Everyone looks more beautiful and more attractive when they are happy and energized. The best beauty regime for women and men is to enjoy life and be true to your heart's desire.

## Win–win

There are two basic styles of negotiation: win–win and win–lose. In win–lose, one party gets what they want but the other loses. Some people, and some salesmen, pride themselves on their ability to get one over on the other party, and rate their deals not on what they have won but on how much they screwed the rest. There are some cut-throat markets where that is appropriate. After all, the best way to survive shark-infested waters is to be a shark. However, in everyday life, win–lose is likely to create buyer's remorse; it undermines trust and it does not create goodwill.

In win–win, both parties feel satisfied with their end of the deal. People will be happy to do business with you if they are happy with the last deal they did. Your job as an influencer is not just to do a deal, but to make the other party feel happy about it. That does not mean you have to split any profit fifty–fifty. It means your job is to make them feel happy about whatever they get, even if they only get 15 per cent.

Experience has taught me to be careful in choosing whom I do business with, but when I do agree to work with people I make sure that everyone has something to feel happy about. A win–win approach to life will make you friends, it will build a valuable and trustworthy network of business acquaintances and it will push you to be creative to ensure everyone will be happy with the outcome.

# IN A NUTSHELL

- Buying is an emotional decision

- An excellent sales person helps customers to make the best decisions

- The best deals are win–win

# NEXT STEPS

When you are selling anything:

➤  Get their attention and build rapport

➤  Find out what they want

➤  Sell the benefits

➤  Inoculate against objections

# 8

·

# THE EVERYDAY
# INFLUENCERS

## The everyday influencers

Our lives are now completely saturated with messages. We have more channels of communication than ever before in human history. There are billions of hours of video on YouTube, there are blogs on every subject under the sun and there are thousands of broadcast and cable TV channels, and newspapers and magazines and radio stations. At the time of writing there are nearly one billion websites. In this chapter we look at the state of current media and see how to navigate the torrents of information and influence that are flooding into our lives.

## It's all different

Everything is changing. You can watch TV programmes whenever you want, you can make video calls all over the world, you access all the information that used to be hidden away in libraries and you can do all your shopping without leaving your home. At no cost whatsoever you can upload a video and your message is available to every single one of the billions of users of the internet. There are YouTubers with a larger audience than the TV networks.

You can pay for things in shops by waving your phone and go online in the middle of a transatlantic flight to play a game, talk to your office or book another plane ticket.

## It's all the same

The channels have changed, but humans are much the same as they were. The biggest change in humans over the last twenty years is that they are more overweight and less fit since so many of them spend so much time in front of a screen. But we still only have one pair of eyes and one pair of ears.

News transmission was once dominated by newspapers. Next television became the dominant medium. Now all the big news channels have a web presence which is becoming more important than their broadcast channels. In theory, of course, we can get our news closer to the sources by searching the internet for primary data and a range of different reports. In practice most people use the channels they already know. Out of all those billion websites on the net the average user visits a total of just 96 different websites per month.

We live in times of swift and revolutionary changes in markets, media and communications. However we can understand a great deal about these changes by looking at three factors: technology, economics and human habits.

## A brave new world?

In the year 2000, social researcher Robert Putnam published *Bowling Alone*, a book about the decline of face-to-face social activity in the USA. It was an enormous meta-study that demonstrated a very strong correlation between the increase in television-watching and the decrease in all forms of civic and social activity in the United States since the 1950s. Since Putnam's book, many people have migrated from the television to the internet but the basic relationship is the same. Our interactions are less often face to face and more often mediated through a screen. People spend a large percentage of their free time either on the internet or watching TV. That has a peculiar effect on the environment in which we live. In large cities it is now commonplace not to know your neighbours and yet to be well informed about conflicts, craziness and natural disasters in distant corners of the globe. The effect of the global reach of media is to bring distant things close, but make us distant from people and things that are physically close.

Back in the 1960s, forty years before Putnam published *Bowling Alone*, Jerry Mander was the head of the leading West Coast advertising agency Freeman, Mander & Gossage. The agency had successful accounts handling British motor cars, Californian wine and prestigious publications like *Scientific American*. Mander was asked to devise an advertising campaign to win support for the preservation of a significant and unspoilt natural wilderness. He was happy to help so he created a campaign. It flopped. He tried again. It flopped again.

Mander was frustrated and he wanted to know why the campaign failed. His frustration eventually drove him to look more closely at television. At that time television was the dominant medium of both entertainment and advertising.

Mander came to realize that television programmes, even those which are not meant to be fiction, distort our perception of what they report.

Although television appears to bring us close to the wonders of nature, it is still actually a flat, electronic screen. The constraints of that screen, and of camera technology, mean that natural scenes that look beautiful in real life, such as forests or coastlines, soon become boring on screen. The muted browns, greys and greens of reality are boring. TV looks better with the bright vibrant colours and straight lines of the manufactured world. Mander could make cars look very good on TV. He struggled, and ultimately failed, to make a wilderness park look interesting.

Mander realized that television distorts the messages it transmits. It favours the selection of antagonistic stories and simplistic analysis. Action and conflict make for interesting viewing. That's why movies and TV drama are packed with incidents, drama and conflict. It is good entertainment. However, the depiction of reality on TV, whether on the news or in documentaries or the weird world of reality TV, is distorted by the same bias towards drama and conflict. That's why there is so much bad news and so little good news on TV. There is no conspiracy to depress us or control us. It is just that bad news is full of conflict and drama and good news is mostly boring. John Smith went for a walk in the park and had fun playing with his kids is boring television. John Smith raided a bank and crashed the getaway car is good television. TV stations in the States monitor police radio channels and send helicopters to film car chases because it will get them viewers.

## What television really sells

With a few exceptions, television stations transmit advertisements. They are selling products to you, the viewer. So we could say TV stations sell goods and services to viewers.

But we can frame, and understand, the same situation differently.

We could say TV stations sell audiences (that's you) to advertisers (the big companies behind the brands that are advertised). When a programme has high viewing figures, all those viewers are watching and listening and are available to be addressed by advertisers. Channels sell eyeballs to brands.

When we see it like that, we understand a great deal. We see that what matters most is viewing figures. TV programmes need to keep you watching and keep you entertained in order to deliver you to those advertisers. Therefore, the job of every TV programme, regardless of whether it is fiction, current affairs, news, reality TV or a documentary, is to take you on such a gripping, emotional journey that you won't turn it off or switch channels and you will tune in again to get the next instalment. That imperative shapes everything that appears on our screens. Nothing is allowed to be boring. Everything must be seen from the most impactful angle. All situations must be framed for maximum emotional engagement. Conflict and difficulties will be exaggerated and complicated issues simplified so that they are easier to follow. Thoughtfulness will be overwhelmed by emotion.

## How your perspective is manipulated

The necessity to capture and retain your attention dominates the structure of TV programmes. The programme is edited to show or create a compelling narrative. Life is messy and every different person has a different perspective but a documentary will be built around a clear storyline even if life is not that simple. News reports focus on gripping sensationalism. When you watch a TV programme you, and a million other viewers, share one single perspective on the topic, that of the editor. Even if you see a selection of talking heads, each expressing a different point of view, one person has selected which heads you will see, and which fragment of what they said will be transmitted.

The best evidence of the effect of TV editing is to watch a programme about a topic, person or place that you know well. I can guarantee you will notice something about it is inaccurate, misleading or completely wrong. I am not trying to be rude to television producers or editors here, because their job is not to depict reality accurately. Their job is to make entertaining programmes. I'm just pointing out what you need to know when you are watching television. You are being influenced by the biases that are built in to every TV programme. Even fictional programmes create subtle distortions in our perceptions of reality. In TV cop shows, 90 per cent of the crimes are solved. In reality, fewer than 10 per cent of crimes are solved.

## The news

A study showed that just 11 per cent of the information transmitted in news programmes was accurate. Coverage of issues is proportionate to the emotional impact they will have, not to their actual impact on the world. Every day there are sadly so many fatal car crashes that almost all of them go unreported. Aeroplane crashes are very, very rare but they are more dramatic so every one of them, even those on the other side of the world, is widely reported.

All commercial TV and internet channels focus on emotions. They know people like to imagine they are rational, but they respond to programmes emotionally. Emotions are the hooks that keep the viewer's attention. Every transmission, whether broadcast or net based, has just a few seconds to capture the viewer's attention and must continue to keep the viewer interested, otherwise they will click, flick or switch away. TV and net channels have a torrent of edits and effects to keep creating compelling visual stimulus.

# The science of propaganda

Perhaps the best-known commentator on media issues of the last couple of decades is linguistics professor Noam Chomsky. Chomsky is famous for his insight:

**Whoever sets the agenda controls the
outcome of the debate.**

Professor Chomsky notes that the media set the agenda for news reporting. For example, by analysing column inches of reporting he noted that AIDS got more than four times more coverage than breast cancer, though even at the height of its devastating peak AIDS killed only a quarter as many people.

Every TV channel, newspaper, radio station and web feed has its own agenda, regardless of whether it carries advertising or not. As Chomsky points out, 'They do this in all sorts of ways, by selection of topic, by distribution of concerns, by emphasis and framing of issues, by filtering of information, by bounding of debate within certain limits. They determine, they select, they shape, they control, they restrict.' Chomsky believes they do this in order to serve the interests of dominant, elite groups in society. I don't know whether or not he is right. I do know, however, that the agenda is definitely determined by the political agenda of the editors or the need to deliver audiences to advertisers.

I used to be asked to take part in shows to debate 'the

dangers of hypnosis'. I knew there was no point in going because the set-up was a negative presupposition. There is plenty of talk about 'balanced debate' but, as long as there are shows with that sort of title, it's more talk than action. I told the producers I would come on the show if they titled the debate: 'The miraculous benefits of hypnosis.'

Every channel of communication has a bias. This is not necessarily a good thing or a bad thing, and it is not at all easy to imagine what a completely unbiased communication would look like. As every single individual only has their own viewpoint, any personal commentary is necessarily biased. And as we saw earlier, a scientific or 'objective' viewpoint specifically excludes the personal emotions on the basis of which humans make choices. As soon as anyone includes emotional responses, they are making a choice which is akin to that of an editor. No single person out there has an objective point of view, and a scientific viewpoint cannot capture the essence of a subjective point of view.

It becomes easier to navigate the media when you know that every communication is biased. You understand more when you understand not just what is said, but also the biases that belong to the person or channel saying it.

Every media channel, including all online media channels, are vulnerable to five biases. These pressures operate regardless of whether or not the writers, reporters or editors are consciously aware of them.

1.  Channels don't want to upset advertisers. If a channel receives income from advertisers, they will veer away from any criticism of that advertiser and tend towards content that is favourable to them. They may occasionally publish controversial reports that give the impression of balance, but overall they will favour the views of their advertisers. If they choose not to do so they will eventually go out of business. Even YouTubers learn to modify their content when they have millions of subscribers and big money advertisers. However loud they talk, money talks louder.

2.  Channels don't want to upset their owners. 90 per cent of the media channels in the USA are owned by just six large corporations. Those corporations also own other commercial and industrial interests, so you will notice that the channels tend to avoid criticism of their owners' other interests.

3.  Channels want to preserve the status quo. If you own 70 per cent of the media channels in the USA, why would you want change? The more powerful any person or corporation is, the more they are investing in keeping things as they are. That doesn't mean there must be a vast conspiracy to mislead the public or oppress minorities. It just means that people and corporations in comfortable dominant positions are not likely to be motivated towards anything that

dilutes their power.

4. Channels want to keep their consumers happy. They want you to keep watching and consuming their advertising. They don't want you to be upset. They don't want you to stop spending money. They don't want you to find anything more interesting to do.

5. All channels want to tell a story. Every programme, video or news report wants to tell a story and that imperative will always come before the facts. Storytelling is the biggest business in the world. Hollywood creates fictional stories, and news channels take everyday life and make stories out of it. News programmes are made to entertain you. If you want all the facts, you will have to search them out yourself.

## Who is running the show?

Whatever the channel, someone somewhere writes the stories and makes the editorial decisions. If you have your own blog or YouTube channel, it's you. If you want to get your message on a TV programme, in a newspaper, on a radio or on a website, there are two people you need to influence. The first is the journalist or reporter, the second is their editor.

I have a friend with a PR company. PR is the business of

arranging the truths in a way that suits your clients' objectives. In other words, the essence of the job is framing and reframing.

My friend's job is to make it easy for journalists to write the story with the framing that he wants. The simplest way is to write it himself and give it to them. That is, in fact, how a huge amount of 'news' is sourced. The proliferation of channels has created a huge thirst for stories and copy to fill the space available, and the pressure of time means that in most cases journalists are happy to cut and paste what they are given.

In some areas, however, the journalists like to do their own research and uncover stories themselves. In those cases, my friend will meet the journalist and give them only a hint of a story or half an idea and then say, 'I'm not sure how that would work.' Then he would let them do the questioning and thinking until they had not only created the story but also believed that they had discovered it themselves.

Nowadays, we are all frustrated by interviews with politicians. The journalists ask trick questions and the politicians appear totally unable to give a simple, straightforward answer. Why don't they just have a normal, reasonable conversation? Once again, the problem is that TV programmes will hold our attention better if conflict is frequent and explanations are simple.

In truth, there are plenty of situations in which governments or politicians do not have or know the answer, but they never say so because they are frightened they will appear indecisive or inadequate.

Remember, whatever the title of the show, its purpose is to hold our attention. Whatever the overt claim, it is not delivering a balanced debate, providing a platform for free speech or educating the public.

In democracies politicians want your votes; in dictatorships they want your obedience. In both cases they go about it the same way. They scare you first and then promise solutions. There is always an enemy to worry about on the one hand and, on the other, the perpetual promise of more jobs, better education and lower crime.

There is pressure on the journalist to create drama by getting the politician to admit an error or mistake. The politician knows that whatever he says is likely to be edited to create the maximum impact. He knows that if he says, 'I'm sorry I made a mistake and the reason is—', regardless of the merits of his reason, his words will probably be edited to, 'I made a mistake.'

Furthermore, an effect of the torrent of information heading our way is that we very quickly forget messages, because we hear another one just moments later. Therefore politicians learn to repeat their message as often as possible to make it stick. The effect is not a conversation in which two people engage thoughtfully in answering each other's questions, but rather a pseudo-conversation in which two people say exactly what they want while merely pretending to listen to the other person.

# The truth about the internet

The internet seems to offer an alternative to the controlled and controlling world of TV. But once again the pressures of the marketplace and the motors of influence are at work. Because it is effectively free to post anything online, people do post anything and everything online. You can access more information than ever before. You can also access more incorrect information and more biased points of view than ever before. The net is awash with bad, biased and misleading information and downright lies. You won't find most of it unless you go looking though, because you are in the bubble.

The internet is not the vast, free, open space that it appears to be when you first log on. Every search engine, every media platform and a lot of hidden software is keeping track of every website you visit and every subject you search. They use that information for two purposes. First, to place adverts in front of you that are related to your activity. Second, to offer you links that you might like. So your news and social-media feeds are biased by your own activity. Very soon you are in a bubble, being fed views similar to your own, and content similarly driven by your likes. Instead of the web increasing your exposure to the views of others and widening your perspective, the bubble isolates you inside a world of like-minded thinkers. Once again, your perspective is being distorted – in this case by feedback from your own behaviour.

## Profiling

The same sort of software that determines your content feed also delivers advertisements. Search engines, social media, apps and websites sell audiences to advertisers, just like TV channels. But now they know a great deal more about the audiences. The data collected from your internet usage is aggregated with that of millions of other users and analysed by algorithms that allow extraordinarily accurate predictions.

An early use of these algorithms was offline, in super-market loyalty schemes. To amass points, customers effectively hand over exact details of which items are bought, by whom, in what combinations, at which time of day. One supermarket noted that men were coming in and buying nappies late at night and deduced that they were being sent out by their tired partners for emergency supplies. The supermarket moved the nappies right next to the beer and sold an awful lot more beer.

Just like loyalty schemes, internet sites know all about your purchases and they also know a great deal more. Analytics can now work out when a woman is pregnant from her internet usage and as a result target her with specific adverts. They know far more than simply that she may buy pregnancy- and baby-related goods. They know also, for example, that she is more likely to change her washing powder when she is pregnant. And how do they know this? By algorithms that have processed millions and millions of data points.

Advertisers know that if your interests overlap with

a large number of their current customers you are a good prospect for their offers, even if you have never heard of their products. The effect is that you are being sold things that you don't yet know you want by companies who already do know that you will want them.

## Astroturfing

There are a good number of large corporations and political interests which care a great deal about what the public thinks about them and are very keen to maintain a good image. Now that the internet has given a voice to anyone and everyone, protestors, complainers and dissenters can get their messages out. Large companies can no longer control their image as easily.

If you or I want to find out if a policy is equitable, if a drug has side effects or if chemical is carcinogenic, we can find evidence in minutes. We have myriad alternatives to the official company website. We can search blogs, we can find independent committees, we can find grassroots action groups and community organizations. We can look up scientific papers and track down surveys and experiments conducted by independent institutions.

It appears there really is a good side to the internet. Well, it appears like that. But big companies with a reputation to defend, and especially big companies with a controversial but lucrative product, know very well what we are likely to do to research their activities. And they have worked out a way to address it. Directly or indirectly they fund community organizations, grassroots action groups, scientific research stations, university departments and independent institutions. And the more they fund them, the more pressure, direct or indirect, exists for those 'independent' groups to be more favourable to their funders.

This process is so well established it has a name. It is called astroturfing, because it is an artificial version of grassroots.

One of the key tools of astroturfers is the scientific study. Very few people bother to look at the details of a scientific study, and even fewer know enough about scientific and statistical procedures to assess its robustness. Such is the respect for science these days that 'scientific study' are two magic words that invoke the powerful influence of authority. In the same way that if you call yourself 'Doctor' very few people will question you, so if you cite a scientific study very few people will question it. They should.

In 2015 journalist Jon Bohannon fooled news channels in more than twenty countries into thinking that chocolate could help weight loss. Jon was originally a scientist by training and knew exactly how to set up a study that was technically valid although in reality meaningless. He recruited a very small sample of subjects and framed his method, his measurement and his statistics to generate a finding that met the criteria for validity, although he and his colleagues knew it was absurd. He measured so many variables that with his tiny sample one of them was likely to deliver a statistically significant result. He found one. With two groups on a controlled diet, the group whose diet included chocolate lost weight marginally faster. Technically valid but in reality bullshit.

As a journalist he knew how to get his results out, and once it hit the mainstream it was picked up and reported all over the world. To this day, there are almost certainly people who read the original report 'Chocolate helps weight-loss' and still believe it because they never read Jon's follow-up piece explaining how he did it.

The technology and the media may have changed but the fundamental strategies of influence remain the same. Social proof works online; consistency, scarcity and association still work online. And more than ever, you can see that every internet user has their own biases and points of view. Strangely, one of the very few things we all have in common is our susceptibility to the universal patterns of influence.

Get used to spotting the patterns of influence because you will see them everywhere. Your insight into these patterns and your own experience are your best guides in interpreting what you hear and see in all the media.

# IN A NUTSHELL

- Media channels sell audiences to advertisers

- Whoever sets the agenda controls the debate

- Every channel has a bias

# NEXT STEPS

➤ Remember there is a lot of good news that does not get reported

➤ If you do research on the internet, dig deep and follow the money

# 9

.

# EVERYDAY HYPNOSIS

## Everyday hypnosis

Hypnosis, to many people, is a power shrouded in mystery. They imagine it is an extraordinary state in which they are helpless or controlled by another person. I have been teaching it for over twenty years now and while I have experienced all of these amazing phenomena, I have also developed the means to explain its mysteries in a clear and easy way.

In the 1950s the early researchers of the modern era believed that hypnosis was a special and separate state of mind that could be recognized by particular experiences. They believed that some people were 'good subjects' because they responded readily to hypnotic commands. Recent researchers, however, have shown that there are some people who are more likely to do what they are told whether they are in 'trance' or not. Nowadays, with a more sophisticated understanding of the power of indirect suggestion, modern hypnotists can be more effective for everyone both with and without trance. As we have reached a better understanding, we can also see that all the phenomena of hypnosis are present in everyday life, even if not to the same intensity as the hypnotic context.

## Hypnotic 'phenomena'

When you watch an interesting programme on TV, your attention is absorbed by the show, you are less aware of your immediate surroundings and you forget about the rest of the world. That absorption shares many characteristics with classical hypnotic trance, such as fixity of gaze and a reduction in the tension of the muscles in the face, yet it is an everyday event.

Have you ever forgotten anything? That is amnesia. Hypnotic amnesia transfers that natural ability to an unexpected reference so that on stage a subject can even be made to forget their own name. Nevertheless, the underlying mechanism is the same as when you come back from shopping and you realize you have forgotten to buy a vital ingredient for dinner.

Have you ever run to catch a train and stubbed your toe but kept running? When you finally sit down on the train, you notice your toe really hurts, but you didn't notice while you were still running for the train. That is natural analgesia, the basis for hypnotic analgesia.

Athletes and racing drivers experience time distortion when they are in a state of peak performance known as 'flow'. We can use this same ability to slow down and speed up time in therapeutic hypnosis to allow people to review and re-contextualize incidents from the past.

Have you ever seen someone in a supermarket lost in thought, trying to decide which cereal to buy? You can see them standing in front of the shelves, with their arm frozen in mid-air while they make up their mind. The person is not consciously holding up their arm and they are unaware of its weight. That ability is the foundation for a hypnotic arm levitation.

Every time an interior designer imagines how a room will look when it is redecorated, they are using our natural capacity for positive hallucination. If you lose your car keys, spend ten minutes looking for them and then find them sitting right in front of you on the table, you have just experienced a natural negative hallucination. Artists use both positive and negative hallucinations and the intense focus of trance when they are in the creative zone.

A hypnotist typically induces behaviours like these outside of their usual context, which causes the subject to realize their abilities to experience their own lives in a very unusual way. Often the changes that the hypnotist induces are accompanied by trance, but it is not always necessary. Trance is just one human capacity among many, and hypnotic phenomena can be induced without trance.

## Understanding hypnosis

Hypnosis can be understood as having two elements: trance and suggestibility. We live in a culture dominated by the activities of the left brain, which are rational, organized and linear. A hypnotist typically elicits right-brain activity, which is creative, artistic, non-linear and emotional. The hypnotist does not use logic for this, but rather association, imagination and metaphor.

Some hypnotic suggestions are verbal, but many are

non-verbal, indirect or metaphorical. They include all the motors of influence that we looked at earlier and a great deal more. When you master the techniques of influence you are every bit as powerful as a hypnotist, because to understand hypnosis is to understand the core of influence.

When I first used hypnosis I was astonished at the sheer power of hypnotic suggestion. There was a kid living next door who had heard about my interest in hypnosis and came to see me because he had a biology exam the next day. He was a far from model pupil and he never did his homework, but I found out that he had been in all his classes. I had just read that day about how the unconscious stores all our experiences so I hypnotized him and told him, 'You will be able to remember all you need.' Two weeks later he came round again. He told me he had failed all his exams except for biology, in which he got an A.

## Trance

Trance is a specific alteration of consciousness. It is typically characterized by a loss of our general reality orientation and a focus of attention on just one or two elements of consciousness. Therapeutic hypnotists often use a focus on breathing or proprioception to focus the mind. Stage hypnotists use their own voice as the focus of attention.

Trance frequently includes relaxation and a very literal

mode of cognition. For example, if a subject is sitting two metres in front of a painting in deep trance and you ask them, 'What is in front of you?' they might answer, 'Nothing,' because directly in front of them is nothing. However, if you ask, 'What is beyond that?' they will say, 'A painting.'

This literalism has been confused in the past with a compulsion to tell the truth. In fact, people in trance are just as likely to lie or fabricate ideas as they are in everyday consciousness. However, hypnosis, if well used, can assist with recall, by means of vivid revival of contextual cues leading to activation of association-based retrieval.

Everyone can go into trance. As I explain to my subjects, we can all relax and we can all daydream and we all know what it is like to imagine things and to be directed towards positive outcomes. I do, however, regularly meet people who believe they cannot be hypnotized. I once saw an eminent surgeon who very much wanted to go into trance, but believed he could not be hypnotized. I asked him about the most complicated operation that he regularly performed. He explained it could take up to five hours, during which time he would be completely concentrated on the task. I asked him whether he would jump if someone accidentally dropped something. 'Of course not,' he replied. So I asked him to close his eyes and, while listening to my voice, to vividly imagine conducting that operation. Within a few minutes he was deeply absorbed in the memory, his consciousness had focused and I was able to induce a deep trance. Incidentally, this is an example of utilization to induce trance. Everyday consciousness is not a single state of awareness. All of us experience different types of trance every day, including daydreaming, highly focused attention, exclusion of sense data and amnesia.

## Suggestibility

Early hypnotists, like Janet and Charcot, observed 'hypnotic phenomena' occurring spontaneously as subjects fell into trance and, wishing to study them further, suggested to the subjects that they repeat the phenomena. Thus the connection was presumed between trance and suggestibility in hypnosis. Up until the 1950s, leading American researchers like Ernest Hildgard believed that trance was an essential component of 'hypnotic phenomena'.

However, people are just as suggestible outside trance as they are in trance. The language we use to influence them is known as hypnotic language patterns or everyday hypnosis. It is possible to massively influence behaviour by the use of suggestion. Suggestions can be direct, indirect, verbal and non-verbal. Sometimes they are associational. For example, the most powerful suggestion in a hypnotic stage show is the name of the show. Every member of the audience comes either to be hypnotized or to witness hypnosis. That creates a massive expectation set, which the hypnotist will activate and use to assist his subjects to go into trance.

Everyday hypnosis is used by politicians, advertisers, cult leaders and sales people all around you every day. All the great orators of history, whether benevolent or malevolent, were great masters of hypnotic language. Some years ago I undertook a study of the speeches of Margaret Thatcher, John F. Kennedy, Adolf Hitler, Tony Blair and Martin Luther King and, while the content differed, the underlying structure was remarkably similar.

Suggestion is not confined to language. When a new drug is created it has to be tested. A typical controlled study will contain two groups. One receives the drug and the other receives a placebo, which is a pill with no active ingredients at all. Very often a good number of the patients who only receive the placebo experience improvements in their condition simply because they believe they are being helped. The authority of the person administering the drug, their title and the context all have an effect, and the pill itself is a powerful suggestion. Research has demonstrated that it is possible to enhance the suggestion just by colour. Red pills have been shown to have a greater effect on pain control than white ones, even though both contain no pain-control chemicals whatsoever.

In a recent experiment, high-performing cyclists were given a new drug. They were told it contained caffeine and another ingredient. Physical performance was measurably increased and one of them went on to beat his personal best performance two times. All the 'drugs' were placebos. Suggestion is very, very powerful indeed.

I am regularly asked, 'Do you use hypnosis to get your own way?' And the answer is yes. I don't put people into trance without their agreement but I do use hypnotic language patterns all the time. I am not, of course, the only person to do so. Sales people, advertisers, orators and religious leaders also use hypnotic language patterns. As you learn more about those patterns here, you become more able to resist them, should you wish, or use them as you want.

## Using hypnosis without trance

Everyday hypnosis includes all the techniques we have already looked at, including the major motors of influence and the patterns we use to sell goods and services, or just ideas. So, if I need to influence someone, first of all I must get their attention. Most of the time, I simply start a conversation. Next I create and build rapport, exactly as I explained in Chapter 3. As I continue to chat I ascertain the values of my subject and note whether they prefer to use visual, auditory or kinaesthetic metaphors.

After I have gained rapport I may use any of the following techniques. I might use them in the order below, but it is not a hard and fast rule. I often change the order, intersperse different elements, and go back and forth between different types of suggestion and different stages of the process. Much of the time I combine many different techniques in a single sentence. In the opening phase I pace my subject's current experience and gradually lead them towards a greater use of imagination and greater awareness of sensory feedback.

## Capture the attention and move it

I often capture attention with a bold or emotive statement or a question. I then build agreement by using a yes set. In my conversation I bring in ideas where we share values and I use words and similes which are similar to those they prefer. I also increasingly use metaphors and sensory and emotive language which address the non-rational right brain. I introduce stories with a vivid sensory element. Listening to stories and firing up the imagination arouses creativity and moves people away from the limitations of logical and rational thinking. I often wish to change people's moods or empower them so I might ask them to think of times they felt confident and happy.

I will ask them to remember a specific time and see it as though through their own eyes. For example, 'Think of a good time now. See again what you saw, hear what you heard and feel what you felt. Make the colours bright and vivid, the sounds clear and sharp and feel how your body feels when you are happy and confident.'

## Yes sets and awareness

Next I might make reference to their ongoing physical experience. I might point out that our everyday awareness has natural limits. For example, normally, although your nervous system is working all the time, you are not aware of feeling at the back of your knees and calves because unless something unusual is happening it is automatically filtered out. However, when I talk about it, it is brought to your attention and you notice the sensation of those parts of your body.

I may draw my subject's attention to other parts of their ongoing physical experience. All the time I point out what is true even though we normally don't notice it. By moving the attention in this way I make what is normal appear unusually vivid. As all my statements are true, I am creating a yes set and allowing the unconscious mind of the subject to relax and trust my descriptions of the world.

I might focus their attention on their breathing with an invitation like this: 'You can notice your breathing, and notice how it rises and falls all by itself, and it carries on whatever you are doing, whatever you are thinking. You can enjoy the way your body breathes for you and enjoy that rhythm which sustains you all day long and all night long.'

Yes set questions about ongoing experience bring the attention to the present moment. For example I can ask, 'As you read these words, you may say them to yourself under your breath or you may read them very fast, and you are free to read as quickly or slowly as you wish, aren't you?' I may follow up with more. 'Are you perhaps curious about the nature of hypnosis? Is it something about which you would like to know more?' I could follow up with a question which builds expectation such as, 'And how do you expect to learn that?'

I can also ask questions and move on before either of us answer them. This causes the answer that automatically springs up to linger longer in the mind of the subject.

## Yes and no

Throughout the ongoing conversation I continue to maintain rapport and build the yes set. People can become bored of saying yes continually so I introduce questions and notions to which the answer is no, although it is still an agreement. Thus they can agree with me, but use the word 'no'. This feels more balanced than a string of yeses one after another.

For example, 'You don't want to waste your time or let people take advantage of you, do you?' or 'I don't believe in rushing into an agreement without checking the small print, do you?'

By alternating yeses and nos throughout the conversation you build deeper agreement while maintaining a good balance between negative and positive language.

## Non-specific references

Our minds automatically seek to make sense of everything we hear. So if I use a word that does not have a specific meaning, the minds of my listeners will automatically look for a meaning for it from their own experience or imagination. Therefore, I can create a powerful and intimate connection with my listeners simply by saying, 'Please imagine your favourite childhood memory. Go back to it now, and see it in your mind's eye as though you are there now. See what you saw, hear what you heard and enjoy exactly how you feel.' This is a powerful suggestion and yet each of us makes sense of those words by remembering different occasions.

I often use words to which people can attach their own meaning. For example, 'I know that you have your own concerns and I very much hope that you will find the resolutions you need as swiftly as possible.' That sentence sounds businesslike, straightforward and well intentioned. But I could say it to anyone about anything. Your 'own concerns' are completely undefined, so the listener will take them as a reference to their own specific concerns, although I, the speaker, might have no idea what they are. Similarly, I don't know what the resolution would be, nor the time frame for 'as swiftly as possible'. However, if my subject does have concerns, this sentence allows me to be very much on their side without any knowledge of the details.

## Hypnotic conjunctions

When I use yes sets, I often link my phrases with conjunctions like 'as', 'while', 'and' and 'during'. While I do this, I allow my subject to agree with my words, and they are free to think whatever they want as I introduce the idea that it is also perhaps to explore new ways of seeing the same things. I might start a seminar, for example, by saying, 'Each of you has come here today for your own specific reasons and I look forward to helping you achieve those goals, yet I also believe there may be even more positive possibilities for you today, and I would like you to be open to learning, both consciously and unconsciously, during our time together so that you continue to benefit from this as you learn more and practise more in the days and weeks to come.'

These longer sentences combined true observations with suggestions or invitations but because they are all in one grammatical entity there is a tendency for the mind to take the whole sentence as true. They also slightly overload the conscious attention and tend to make the subject pick up on the last element as the resolution or meaning of the sentence.

## Using metaphors and stories

Everyday language is full of metaphor. A metaphor is the figure of speech in which a term is used in a context to which it is not literally applicable in order to emphasize a quality or resemblance. For example, 'He came to the meeting with a lorry load of ideas.' We don't understand that he drove a lorry into the meeting. It just means he brought a very large number of ideas. Simile is the figure of speech in which comparison is used for the same effect, for example, 'She drove like a bat out of hell.'

In a hypnotic conversation I often use metaphors and similes for two reasons. First, they activate the emotional, non-rational right-brain. Second, a good metaphor will induce your subject to visualize the scene, thus encouraging them to use their own imagination. The metaphor can also act as an indirect suggestion. I can tell a metaphorical story about how a child learns effortlessly every day simply by observing the world around them and playing games, and as you hear, your unconscious mind will automatically register the parts of that story that pertain to you.

I often work with people by talking about someone else. I explain that the other person did this, this and this and I create a road map for how it will be for them. I have helped a lot of people overcome heartbreak. Often they have been told well-intentioned, logical ideas like, 'There are plenty more fish in the sea', but it just reinforces their bad feeling because they are missing the specific person they have just lost. So I pace them. I say something like, 'You feel sad. That's understandable,' and I tell them of my own experience of feeling heartbroken. I remember sitting in this very room feeling really down and believing the pain would never stop. Just like you, I didn't know when it would get better. But it did. At first I didn't notice and I didn't understand how it happened and it was only later that I remembered that I had been in love before, and heartbroken before, and I noticed that only when I felt better.

This is the difference between logic and storytelling. If we try to use logic, people can use their left-brain thinking to argue with us but when we tell stories they can join us in the feeling of the story. We can use this in business or family situations by telling stories that illustrate what we want, and then moving on without discussing it any more. People will find the meanings they need in the stories we tell. I worked with a young woman a couple of times. After dealing with some traumatic issues in the first session, I told a story to lighten the atmosphere. When she came to see me the next week she said, 'Thank you. I know why you told me that story. I've been remembering it all week and it really helped.' Actually I had not realized how helpful that story could be, but my unconscious mind was cleverer than I was and prompted me to tell the story.

## Presuppositions

The single most important hypnotic language patterns are presuppositions. You can use them throughout your use of influence. You can introduce them with hypnotic conjunctions or as sub-clauses before yes sets. Presuppositions frame a statement or request in such a way that another idea is taken for granted. The following are presuppositions.

If you ask your children, 'Do you want to put on your pyjamas before or after you brush your teeth?' you are giving them a choice about when to brush their teeth. However, you have presupposed that they will put on their pyjamas.

A sales person might say, 'I can see you are looking for a suit today, and when you spend that much money it is important that you find something you will be really happy with. Please tell me the sort of thing you are looking for and let's find what is right for you. Try it on and think about it, and take your time to make up your mind before you buy. When you have decided there is something you like, I will do my best to get a good deal for you.' The sales person finishes with a clear offer which gives a feeling of being very open and even-handed, but the speech beforehand is loaded with presuppositions.

Excellent persuaders, whether we are talking about salesmen, mothers, politicians or preachers, all master the artful use of presupposition. Some presuppositions can be very unfortunate. I always wince when I hear a mother who snaps at her child, 'Why do you always misbehave?' She is implying to her child that their behaviour is permanent and she is embedding a suggestion that is likely to produce bad behaviour in the future.

Presuppositions are influential because the listener has to accept whatever is presupposed in your sentence in order to make sense of it. So, for example, when I say, 'If he's as funny as she is, we'll all be laughing,' you have to accept that she's funny. Even if you didn't think she was funny, you momentarily accept that she is in order to understand my remark.

Presuppositions can appear very natural and harmless. If you are buying a new laptop and the sales person asks, 'Before you choose which machine you'd like, may I ask you a few more questions?' they appear very helpful. At the same time there is a presupposition that you will choose a machine from the selection you have been shown, and an implication that you will buy it.

I like to introduce presuppositions into the flow of the conversation and let their effect accumulate.

If you put three presuppositions in a row the mind tends to accept the fourth one uncritically because it is busy processing the implications of the earlier ones. The more you practise doing this the more easy you will find it, and obviously I cannot know exactly when you will master the technique but I do know that after you have done so you will have greatly enhanced your ability to be influential in everyday conversations.

## Using presuppositions

Presuppositions are the secret language of hypnosis because in order to make sense out of the sentence, people have to accept at some level of their thinking that it is all true. When your language is loaded with presuppositions, it tends to drive the thinking of whoever you are talking to in a particular direction. I never rely on a single presupposition to create the effect I desire. I use an avalanche of presuppositions to create an unstoppable force. Each suggestion in the avalanche is like a single snowflake, light, delicate and almost weightless, but together they create a huge force.

The real power of presupposition is where it is placed. I must have attention and rapport first and then I introduce presuppositions. For example, in a sales situation you could say, 'You are looking for a new machine, and nowadays manufacturers know that everyone wants good value and reliability. I also understand you need to keep your overheads down.' Three pacing statements build rapport, then you can introduce presuppositions.

'As you are looking round, feel free to ask any questions you want. I don't know which features are most important to you, but whether or not you have made up your mind yet, I'm happy to give you any information you may need.'

After at least three presuppositions you introduce the one that delivers your goal. 'Whether you decide on this machine or one of our other models is not important, what is important is that you make the right choice.' In this presupposition, the emphasis of the sentence is on 'the right choice' but the presupposition is that you, the customer, will choose one of their products.

If I am talking to someone about going on a date I might say, 'I don't know about you, but I like to have fun when I go out. I'm quite easy-going – when you are having a good time it doesn't matter what we are doing. I don't even know what sort of things you are into, but we get on well so it could be a good night.'

If I am opening negotiations I can say, 'We are all here to find a good deal and make sure that we get the best possible outcome. When we have heard all the propositions and acknowledged the elements we are agreed on, it may take a bit more work and goodwill to reach an agreement.'

In order to create presuppositions, first have clearly in your mind the outcome you want to deliver, then build a series of presuppositions that lead towards it. Build rapport and ensure that you maintain it. As you practise you will find that it becomes easier, and when your presuppositions are more subtle, success comes more easily. You can also use presuppositions to set up compliance with a direct suggestion. Furthermore, the more you practise creating presuppositions, the more easily you will spot them when they are used on you.

When you re-read this book you will find that there are many presuppositions that help you move towards greater competence and influence. When you use presuppositions yourself, take your time. You don't have to put them all together in successive sentences, you can just drop a few into your conversation. I always take time to establish that the subject is accepting my presuppositions before I deliver the core suggestions I wish them to take on board. I prefer to use very open and permissive language for presuppositions. For example, 'You picked up this book for a reason, and I don't know when you will finish reading it, but I would be interested to know which chapter you found most useful and how many differences you notice when you get used to your greater power to influence people.' That statement, which ostensibly is about what I don't know, presupposes that:

**You will finish reading this book.**
**You will find some or all of the chapters useful.**
**You will find one of the chapters most useful.**
**You will feel at ease with your new powers of influence.**

## PRACTICE

1. Take your time to re-reread this chapter and make a note of each category of hypnotic language pattern.

2. Continue to practise the rapport skills and yes sets that you have learned in Chapters 3 and 4.

3. Every day, create and write down 3 sentences containing examples of each of the following:

   Non-specific references

   Hypnotic conjunctions

   Influential metaphors ( or a metaphorical story)

   Presuppositions

4. Do this every day for at least one week. Do not worry at all if at first your sentences and stories seem clunky or stupid. Practise every day and over time they will become more and more natural and it will be easier and easier.

When you first start to use hypnotic language you may feel clumsy. The solution is simply to practise. After a while you will find yourself using it naturally as you get your own way more often, and as you listen to the trance your unconscious mind will notice and install hypnotic language patterns as you both experience their benefits.

# IN A NUTSHELL

- Hypnotic phenomena occur naturally every day

- The mind will automatically make sense of every non-specific reference

- Three presuppositions in a row create a compelling set

# NEXT STEPS

➤ Write out your examples of hypnotic language patterns every day

➤ Do this every day for at least one week

➤ At the end of the week practise using them in an everyday conversation with a friend

➤ Ask your friend for feedback and act on it

➤ Carry on writing, practising and using all these patterns until you feel completely at ease with all of them and notice you are introducing them into your speech without conscious effort

# 10

·

# THE CORE
# OF CHARISMA

## The core of charisma

We've all been bored. We all know what it is like to hear someone pretending to be really enthusiastic but we know it is just an act. We also know what it is like to be touched, moved and inspired. But what exactly is different?

The difference is emotional honesty. When people speak from the heart, they are magnetic. Therefore one of the most powerful pieces of advice I can give you can be said in four words:

**Be true to yourself.**

In a way it is crazy that we should ever need such advice. People have different aspects of themselves, and behave differently in different circumstances, but surely all of these form the whole of our characters. Even if someone tells a lie, they've chosen to do it so are being true to their own choice.

Nonetheless we do have a sense, however vague, of what 'Be true to yourself' means. I have many different styles of behaviour. I adapt to the company I am in, but whatever the language, whatever the style, if I am true to my feelings and values I am true to myself.

So does 'Be true to yourself' just mean, 'Don't lie'? That is certainly a start, but there is more to it. It is bad enough when human beings lie to others, but when people lie to themselves they are really in trouble.

It is all to do with the make-up of human beings. Human beings have free will. We are always choosing what to do and, in a sense, how to be ourselves. We can choose either to acknowledge what we really feel, or we can choose to deny it and pretend to feel something else. If a person denies what they are feeling it creates stress and incongruity in the non-verbal signalling. They are pulled in two different directions. When you acknowledge your own feelings, even if they are difficult or uncomfortable, you are true to yourself. When you acknowledge your feelings and also live by your values, you have integrity and authenticity.

## Congruence

The authentic self is honest, vulnerable and powerful. Becoming authentic is not about changing your essence or being 'better'. It is about getting rid of the denial, evasion and distortion generated by fear and defensiveness. When we are authentic we don't deny any feeling or parts of ourselves. Nor do we allow ourselves to be overwhelmed by one particular single emotion. Our feelings are, in part, perceptions. When we accept them we accept the message they are delivering, so the feeling changes or disappears. Sometimes this happens in an instant, sometimes it takes longer.

We are more powerful because all our energies are aligned and pointing in the same direction and we are free because we are not held back by attachment to a particular feeling or belief. We are congruent. In moments of authenticity we embrace the entirety of our human experience. This fullness of humanity is a crucial component of charisma.

The following story illustrates this point well. A friend attended a new-age workshop at which a tired and mousy-looking woman said that she was fed up of cooking for her husband's girlfriends. In the past she had agreed to an open relationship, so she felt embarrassed to admit what she felt. Little by little she acknowledged her true feelings and uncovered more and more of them. As she did so, she became completely clear about what she really felt and wanted. She had made a mistake in agreeing to an open relationship. She wanted her husband to be faithful or to leave, and she didn't want to see any more girlfriends, let alone cook for them.

That was perhaps no surprise. What was surprising and amazing was how her appearance completely transformed as she owned what she really felt. The mousy woman disappeared and she became powerful, exciting, vibrant and sexy. It was as though a totally different woman had appeared.

## Amplification

When we speak authentically all our non-verbal communication is congruent with our words. Our words are in harmony with our whole physiological state and that massively amplifies the impact of what we say.

We don't have to wait to be perfect to do this. We don't need to have sorted out every problem and be focused on a single concept. The requirement is just to be honest with ourselves, so that we acknowledge inner conflicts rather than deny them. That means listening to all our feelings and learning from them – not dividing them into right and wrong.

We humans are not objects, we are an ongoing process, so if I accept challenging feelings or uncomfortable truths it doesn't mean I am stuck with them for ever. It means I accept where I am, and if I want to change that is the best place to start. Authenticity amplifies your power.

## The power of vulnerability

There are some situations in which our vulnerability is our greatest strength. Many years ago, a man came to see me because he was frustrated at not getting a girlfriend. He had recently met a woman he really admired and fancied, but he simply didn't know what to do. He felt that he was just an average guy and had nothing to offer to such a wonderful woman. He had not even dared yet to ask her out on a date. He believed that would be the most difficult thing he could imagine, and the thought of the rejection and embarrassment he feared was overwhelmingly horrible.

'Well,' I said, 'you've got one thing to offer that is

extraordinary. If you ask her out, you are showing her that you are willing to go through the most difficult thing you can imagine for her. That's pretty big.'

They went out on a date.

His willingness to show his vulnerability was massively influential. Influence and charisma are not all about glory and power, sometimes their power comes from sharing our weaknesses. In fact, vulnerability is the price of love. It is only because I am open enough to get hurt that I am open enough to give and receive love.

## Checklist

I have a set of questions which help me be authentic and deliver my message powerfully. If I have been busy or stressed and I have an important meeting, I take a few moments to ground myself and to ask these questions.

### 1. Am I being honest?

Honesty is slightly more complicated than it seems. Honesty does not mean full disclosure of every fact. You don't have to tell everyone everything you know, and you can't claim to be objective. Honesty simply means being as truthful as you can. It means acknowledging your feelings to yourself, even if you don't express them out loud. If you feel frightened, acknowledge it to yourself, even when you don't intend to tell anyone else. You can change that feeling, but only after you have first accepted it.

## 2. Am I being direct?

Am I saying what I mean? If I have a worry or a concern, am I raising it with the person it involves? Or am I displacing my concern? Am I focusing on a petty issue because I am really worried about something much more important? We all have a tendency to want to avoid difficult conversations, but if we do so for too long our feelings come out indirectly. It may take courage, it may take two or three attempts, but your influence will be all the more powerful when you say what is really on your mind.

## 3. Is this what I want, or is it what I believe I *should* want?

Life is peppered with 'shoulds' – and they all refer to some external authority. You 'should' be polite, you 'should' dress a certain way, you 'should' remember your partner's birthday. All of these 'shoulds' come from social conventions or laws and many of them are sensible and useful, for example, you 'should' drive on the correct side of the road. But in more personal matters we all inherit 'shoulds' that may no longer be applicable, and we meet other people who assume their 'shoulds' should be our 'shoulds'. Whenever you find yourself doing or saying something because you feel you 'should' do it, check with yourself. Do I, today, agree with this 'should'?

## 4. Am I being congruent with my own values?

Am I saying or advocating something I personally value? If I am, my advocacy is all the more powerful because all my non-verbal communication will be congruent with my speech.

If I am not, do I really want to advocate it? Sometimes when we ask this question it will reveal that it is time to change course or step back from an involvement. I had a friend who was the chairman of a committee. Two members had an ongoing dispute about using confidential data. He confided in me that he didn't agree with either side, and neither side was willing to compromise. His proposals had all been rejected and none of the alternatives were congruent with his values. As he was speaking, he realized the answer to his problem was to resign. It wasn't his problem and they could sort it out among themselves. He resigned and felt better immediately.

## 5. Am I people-pleasing?

Most of us like to be liked, but for some people it is too important. People who do not love themselves seek to feel good by getting others to like them instead. When you have thoroughly worked the exercises in Chapter 2 you will feel great in yourself and you will not be reliant on the liking of others. Nonetheless, even those of us who no longer crave other people's approval may still have a habit of seeking it. Check that your own motivation is not just seeking the approval of others. I find it useful from time to time to remind myself that whatever I do there will always be three types of people in the world: those who love me, those who hate me and those who don't give a damn. Nearly everyone in the world is in the last category and, however nice I am, there will always be some in the middle category – even if only because I got the parking space they were after. And the people I really need to cherish and be grateful for every day are in the first category. There is no point in using the approval of others to feel good. The key is to be true to your own values.

## 6. Have I got a secondary agenda?

A secondary agenda is an intention which is hidden behind what you appear to be doing.

There is nothing wrong with having a secondary agenda. But in order to be influential you must not be embarrassed about it, and you must be willing and able to discuss it if it comes up.

A friend told me two stories that illustrate this. Aged sixteen he went to a very smart party in a posh part of town where he knew only a few of the guests. He noticed a stunning pair of girls, gathered his courage and approached one of them. 'Do you know so-and-so?' he asked, blushing. The other one turned to her friend and said, 'I think he fancies you.' He did of course fancy her, but was too embarrassed to say so. My friend felt crushed and retreated. Ten years later he found himself in a library sitting opposite a beautiful woman reading Montaigne in the original French. 'Are you

French?' he asked. '*Non,*' she replied. Without missing a beat he brought up his secondary agenda: 'Would you have lunch with me?' he asked. '*Oui,*' she replied.

## 7. Am I being defensive?

If someone is being defensive, they have perceived someone else's actions as an attack, and they have reacted to it. They may react with outrage, or self-righteous anger, with coldness or any number of aggressive or defensive strategies, but in every case they have let someone else set the agenda.

This is not a powerful move, and there are three better alternatives. The first, and generally I prefer this, is to reframe the other person's behaviour. I can see their actions as a mistake, an accident, an unfortunate weakness, a cry for help, a misunderstanding or even a clumsy attempt at cooperation. If the person was not really attacking me, this allows us to settle the matter amicably. If they were really attacking me, these reframes give me a great deal of room to manoeuvre.

The second alternative is to assert my own agenda and make clear exactly what I want or expect from that other person. This is neither defence nor attack but an explicit statement of what I want or require.

Finally the third, and my least favourite, is to attack the person and to do so in my own way on my own terms. The saying goes that 'the best form of defence is attack' but for me it is a last resort. Having said that, if I do it, I do the job properly.

## 8. Am I avoiding an uncomfortable feeling or an inconvenient truth?

This one is tricky. Most of the time we run our lives with habits so that we don't have to make choices all the time. Effectively this means we choose, by default, to carry on with habits and then every now and then we choose a change of direction. This means we can hold an idea about ourselves (or anyone else) and keep believing it, even after it is no longer true.

If the truth is painful, then people may be motivated to avoid it and cling to a more comforting interpretation of reality.

If it really isn't true, then gradually a pressure will build up because of the widening gap between reality and the belief. Then we have another choice: do we admit we were wrong, and accept the painful feeling that might go with that, or do we work hard to buttress our mistaken belief?

Often people can get a hint of whether they are avoiding something from a sense of stress or excessive intensity. I check myself by trying to relax. If something stops me, I know I have to check it out.

Authenticity is not intensity or obsession. People who appear or act obsessively or fanatically are frequently avoiding uncomfortable feelings or inconvenient truths.

## Deceit

Good influencers have much in common. They are flexible, confident, goal-oriented and optimistic. However, although we have so much in common, we all have our own unique characters. I have suggested here that good influencers are always true to themselves. To be accurate, that is not always true. There are some highly influential people who are downright deceitful. More than one sales trainer has said, half in jest and half in earnest, 'The key to influence is authenticity. If you can fake that, you're in.'

The advantage of authenticity and of being honest with yourself is that it helps you defend yourself against influential frauds. The more honest you are with yourself, the more you will be accurate in your assessment of other people. That's why it is said, 'You can't cheat an honest man.'

There is a widespread type of fraud now commonly practised via email known as the '419er' after the Nigerian Law that it contravenes. It takes the form of someone claiming they can gain access to hundreds of millions of dollars, but asking for help in setting up a bank account in order to release the money. Anyone foolish enough to reply will be asked to send a 'small' sum, such as ten thousand dollars, to set up the required bank account. Ten thousand dollars is not a small sum. It only appears small by comparison to hundreds of millions of dollars (see Framing in Chapter 5). The deal is always in some way shady or illegal, so once a fool is involved they are deterred from seeking outside help or advice. And of course a totally honest person would not get involved in appropriating money that does not belong to them in the first place. Being honest will protect you from 419ers and other fraudsters.

But it is not always that simple. I have a friend who is rigorously honest, and yet has been cheated more than once by people she considered friends. How did that happen? It turned out that she knew they were unreliable, but she felt she should be generous and she should believe what they told her. Two 'should's. She was avoiding acknowledging the painful truth that those particular friends were not trustworthy. She saw her actions as forgiving and charitable, but because she chose to ignore her own misgivings and distrust, she was cheated.

## Ongoing process

Our existence is a continuous process of change. Every decision we make affects the person we are becoming. My friend, for example, has gradually learned to put better boundaries in place with people she cannot trust.

When we start to be more honest about what we really feel, we remove the ideas, beliefs or habits that were blocking our power. It may not appear very dramatic from the outside, but a lot happens on the inside.

False habits or beliefs that block your power were nearly all installed as a form of self-defence in an early episode of your life. For example, people with low self-esteem may have been brought up in an environment where their value was undermined or attacked. They learned to keep their heads down to avoid more attacks.

So nowadays, as you recognize your own feelings, it can be a moving and painful process to acknowledge the pains of the past before you let them go.

You will find, however, that the better you know yourself, the easier it is to read other people. You will educate your instincts and learn to avoid certain people. Sometimes I meet people who appear charming and talented, but I feel there is something not quite right. Often I don't know what it is and I couldn't tell you what bothers me. I have worked with quite a few such people in the past. And I have, like my friend, believed that I 'should' trust them and give them a chance. I have lived to regret it. Nowadays, if I get those feelings, I try not to get involved. Even if I don't yet know as much as my own unconscious, experience tells me it is worth trusting the signals it is giving me.

## Core

Authenticity is the core of charisma. Authenticity means you speak from the heart and you are true to your own values. When you are that straightforward, sometimes you can get exactly what you want just by asking. Complete honesty massively increases the chances of people agreeing to your requests.

Maintaining your authenticity is an ongoing challenge, and an extremely rewarding one. It is also the basis for the charisma which you will unleash in the next chapter.

# IN A NUTSHELL

- Authenticity amplifies your authority

- Authenticity is sometimes painful, but always rewarding

- Authenticity is an essential ingredient of charisma

# NEXT STEPS

➤ We are all 'work in progress', so use the checklist to maintain your authenticity

➤ Seek out authenticity in others

# 11
·
# THE CHARISMA FORMULA

## The charisma formula

In Hollywood they say there is a difference between an actor and a movie star. An actor will come on screen and do a great job. A movie star comes on screen and you can't take your eyes off them. Some movie stars only light up when they are in front of a camera. Others have it all the time. Sean Connery and Jack Nicholson are just as charismatic in real life as they are on screen. In the UK we have charismatic TV stars like Jamie Oliver, Jeremy Clarkson and Simon Cowell, and all of them are just the same off screen as on. These charismatic people seem to have a magic about them. I was astonished when I stumbled across techniques which everyone can use to become charismatic.

Charisma is like luck. All of us know of people who seem to be lucky, but until recently scientists believed that luck was random chance. That has all changed. Professor Wiseman's experiments proved there are factors hidden in our perceptual filters that make some people lucky and other people unlucky. When you change yourself you change your luck. I believe that in the same way charisma is learnable. You can change yourself and become attractive, likeable and powerful. You can have charisma.

We have the formula which will make you more interesting to other people, more fascinating and more attractive. We can bring out your unique human qualities. I used this process with an actor friend and, at a photo shoot the next week, the photographer immediately asked him, 'What's happened?' All the photographs had a new intensity. I worked with a television broadcaster who went home and her husband spontaneously remarked she looked different and somehow younger. An actress I worked with found herself getting hit on so much she asked me whether I could undo the process. I had to teach her how to tone it down. Another friend is not famous but she wanted to know what it felt like for a week. She was sure all famous people felt so confident and powerful. We used this technique to give her charisma and suddenly she found people kept saying, 'I'm sure I know you from TV,' and she was being asked for autographs. I will explain the steps of this formula in this chapter but I want to emphasize straight away that the written part is just to help you when you practise it later on. You must start by doing it with me on the video download until you are fully proficient.

## Sceptical

We see charisma in other people. We see people who look cool, attractive, striking, powerful, hypnotic and . . . something extra which we can't define. We see it but we can't see how they are doing it. That person is the centre of attention, the magnet, the brightest star in the room.

When I told people I could make them charismatic like that, they didn't believe me, and I don't expect you to believe me right now. I imagine you would like to believe me and you want to believe me, but until you have some real, live experience it is unlikely that you do believe.

There are two good reasons to be sceptical. The first is that becoming charismatic is a big achievement. If it was easy, wouldn't everyone do it? The second is to do with charisma itself. At the heart of charisma is something mysterious, something indefinable, alluring and yet just beyond our grasp. Mystery is an integral part of charisma, so it appears strange that you can learn it, or teach it, in the same way that you can learn to play tennis, speak French or improve your public speaking.

It has been a long process to unpack and codify charisma and to make an easy-to-understand system that works. It has taken years of work and observation to analyse it and explain it. And, as you will see, the crucial breakthrough was in fact a lucky accident.

Now we have a reliable method. The more you work it, the more you get. Your charisma could be as bright as a shining star or as gentle as the breeze. You can be larger than life or quietly magnetic. I must also say that releasing your charisma may be quite a challenging task. Some of you will find it easy, others may have more work to do. It all depends on your starting point and your own unique circumstances.

## Switching it on

Some charismatic people seem to be able to switch it on and off. One moment they are glowing with energy and passion. The next they switch it off and just fade into the crowd.

There is a famous story of Marilyn Monroe walking through New York with a friend. The friend remarked that no one was paying them any attention, even though Marilyn was by then a famous movie star. 'That's because I'm Norma Jean,' said Marilyn. 'Watch this.' And she turned it on. Within a few minutes they were mobbed. Marilyn was able to do that because she already had years of experience of being in public and being the centre of attention.

The rest of us need to build up the elements of charisma over time. Charisma is not just a knack that you can learn and then repeat over and over again like a conjuring trick. Charisma happens differently in different circumstances. You must adapt to each context you face.

Charisma is not a skill, although you will need skills to project it. Charisma is not just styling, although you can banish it with styling mistakes. Charisma is not celebrity, although celebrities can be charismatic and charismatic people can become celebrities.

Charisma is completely personal and yet universally understood. Charisma takes work to achieve, yet ultimately it is something beyond your control. At the highest level it is a gift from the universe.

## Quality

It is not enough to be famous, or powerful, or beautiful or talented. There are all sorts of alluring performers' tricks to catch the attention and captivate an audience, but while they can highlight and transmit charisma, charisma is not a trick, it is something much deeper. Your charisma is a quality of your being. It is grounded in who you are. When you develop your charisma, you will be developing your whole being.

True charisma includes a sense of humility, because charisma is not egocentric. Essentially charisma is a quality of how you are perceived, and that is more important than how you feel. Simon Cowell received a piece of advice from his dad that he tells me he always remembers. His dad told him, 'Remember, everyone has a sign above their head saying *Make me feel important.*' I believe that is why he has such a compelling presence. Truly charismatic people are not actually interested in their own importance. Their attractiveness and power is simply a natural consequence of their authenticity, focus and internal balance. They really focus on the task at hand and what is needed by the people around them.

## Positive focus

Charisma is founded in your being, but it is manifest in your effect on other people. When you are charismatic, people are drawn to you. You make them feel uplifted by driving them into positive states. One of the simplest ways to elicit positive states in others is to ask them questions, because whenever we hear a question we feel the pressure of social proof pushing us to answer. I like to ask:

**Who or what in your life makes you happiest?**
**What is it about them that makes you happy?**
**What is your favourite time of the year?**
**What do you love most about it?**
**What is your favourite childhood memory?**
**How does it make you feel?**

If the context is appropriate, questions like this can lift people's spirits in moments. I like to find out what people find most exciting, what they most enjoy doing and what is their heart's desire. With all of these questions I ask for more and more detail so that the person becomes more absorbed in the memory and the associated state becomes stronger and stronger.

I am always seeking clues as to what people love and what makes them feel loved. This inner intention is transmitted by my non-verbal communication and influences people to focus on the same things. People may not know consciously why they feel good, but they do. Often people spontaneously start to speak of their passion and hopes and they reinforce the feelings that have been seeded by my non-verbal communication.

## Styling

Some people are embarrassed to talk about the basics of presentation, but a good close friend should tell you if you need to know. So I'm going to tell you. Just putting on a clean shirt and having fresh breath won't make you charismatic, but shabby clothes or bad breath can undermine you.

Whenever you are going to be on show – on stage, on television, at work, or any time in your regular life that you want to be at the peak of your performance – make sure that everything you wear feels good and looks good. Make sure you are dressed well and you have a good haircut. Guys should have the right shave and women should have just the right make-up. The effect of getting every one of these little details right is that you will feel better about yourself and that will be transmitted to your audience.

Having said that, context is significant. If there has been a major disaster, the state of your clothing is not important. If you have charisma you can stand up, grab people's attention and organize a rescue effort. No one cares whether your T-shirt is freshly laundered.

In the showbiz parts of Los Angeles, everyone always has a good haircut, but it doesn't stop there. If you are serious about status you should have a personal stylist, or at least look as though you do.

The rest of the world isn't as obsessed with appearance as LA. The basic requirement is to make sure that your clothing makes you feel good and is not off-putting to others. Fancy clothes won't make you charismatic, but you have to dress so that your clothes do not detract from the effect you intend. It doesn't matter where you are on the spectrum from sober to sexy. The choice is yours. There are no hard and fast rules. The key to understanding what works for you is to pay attention to the feedback. If people pay attention to you and congratulate you that's great. If you don't get any compliments it's probably time to change. And if the whole styling thing is not your thing, just ask a friend whose taste you admire and trust to help you out.

## Performance

When you are charismatic people pay attention to you. If you have an audience, that makes you a performer. You don't need a stage or lighting or a fancy costume. You are a performer as soon as you have caught their attention. What next? Performing is like cooking. You can be super fancy or you can be super simple, but what makes it good cooking is getting the basics right.

## Own the space

First of all, own the space. That means act like this space, right here, feels like home to you. You are comfortable, you know your way around. If you appear nervous, your audience will feel nervous. When you are comfortable, they can relax.

To make yourself comfortable, take the time to look around and notice how you feel in this place and how other people feel to you. If you have something urgent and important to say – in fact, especially if you have something urgent and important to say – don't rush. Wait. It is easy to be caught in the excitement of your ideas or your new project or the story you have to tell. Don't get lost in it. Bring your attention to how your body feels, to what you see, hear and feel around you.

With your attention in the present you can build rapport with individuals and reach out to crowds. Pause, look around you and notice what you feel without any judgement, and even if you don't say a word out loud, imagine in your heart that you are saying 'hello' to everyone in the room.

## On stage

If I am going to give a performance or presentation in a large auditorium, I use a technique from the world of acting. I go onstage before the audience arrives. I stand in the middle of the stage and imagine a copy of myself on the right-hand end of the back row of the theatre. I imagine another copy of myself in the centre of that row and a third on the left-hand end of the row. Then I imagine another copy on the right-hand end of the centre row, one in the middle and one at the left-hand end. Along with the front row, just in front of the stage where I am standing, they mark out the whole space of the theatre. When I walk out on stage later I am aware that I sent out those markers and somehow I feel my energy fill the auditorium. I don't know how that works but it is so powerful I suggest you try it and feel it yourself.

When you are on a stage in a theatre there is a technique to looking natural. First of all, you have to get used to being dazzled. If there is a spotlight shining on you, you don't squint or shade your eyes. You don't comment on the fact that you can't see your audience. You are used to it so you ignore it.

Second, you make sure that your audience can see you. You face them. And when you are having a conversation with one other person on stage, you don't sit or stand facing each other. You position yourselves at forty-five degrees so that the audience can see both of you.

Third, you don't fidget and you don't look down. You move less and when you do move you do so deliberately and then you stop. That sounds artificial, but it looks more natural.

## Voice

Charismatic people may be powerful and professional but they are not necessarily slick. Charismatic people speak from the heart and that engages the hearts of the audience. Speaking to an audience is not the same as an ordinary conversation. With an audience you have to act differently even if you want to give the impression of a cosy chat with friends. You must learn to eliminate all the 'ums' and 'ers' you might use normally. With an audience every 'um' and 'er' sounds bigger and louder and dumber than it does in a one-to-one situation. It is fine to pause, or take time to think, but when you do it just pause and say nothing.

Next reduce the swear words. I'm not being prudish.

Personally I choose to use profanity on occasion for emphasis but I am selective where and when I do so. In a presentation or talk, too many profanities can sound strangely boring. Once upon a time they might have been shocking, but that's not true any more. Also, somewhat counter-intuitively, they sound weak. In everyday speech people use them for comedy, to emphasize an opinion or to grab someone's attention. But when you have an audience, people are already listening so you don't need to make them listen more. Swearing sounds as if you have lost control rather than being in control.

## Volume

Next, get used to adjusting your voice to your context. You raise your voice, or you lower it, to make sure that everyone can hear you, but no one feels deafened. Speaking louder means using the resonance of your chest, it doesn't mean shouting. Nobody should need to strain to hear you. If you have developed a voice that is usually loud you may have to learn to speak more quietly.

Now you have to deal with the acoustics and the size of your audience. Generally speaking, in a large space you need to speak a little slower and more clearly. If you are using a microphone you will need to hold it at the correct distance from your mouth. Pay attention to the acoustics. If they are poor you will need to speak more slowly and you will have to articulate more clearly.

Does that all sound complicated? If you are new to it all, how do you learn all this? There is a simple solution. If you are not sure whether you can be heard and understood, just ask. When you own the space, you are no longer shy about making sure everyone is comfortable. Ask the people at the back if they can hear you clearly, and adjust your volume, speed and diction until they say yes!

## Speaking with authority

Now your speech is clear, the volume is appropriate and your timing is right. Everyone is listening. How do you convey your authority? Research has shown that one simple change makes an enormous difference: downward inflection.

Nowadays many people let their voice rise at the end of a sentence. It is partly a habit that has spread through imitation, but it is also a signal to the unconscious to defuse threats. As the voice rises at the end of a sentence it adds a slight feeling of indefiniteness or uncertainty that lets the other party know that they are free to offer a different point of view. If you want to have a definitive effect on an audience you need to do the opposite. Practise making a downward inflection at the end of your sentences. It is simple, subtle and highly effective.

## INFLECTION

1. Stop reading now. Say some short, simple sentences and make a clear downward inflection at the end.

2. Start with these:

   I want to tell you a story.

   I have something really fascinating to tell you.

3. Say these sentences and a couple more of your own 5 times in a row so that you get the inflection loud and clear.

   Now record yourself saying them.

4. Listen back, and repeat the process until you have a clear, firm downward inflection at the end of each sentence and you can hear that your voice sounds authoritative.

## Internal state

Your internal state is transmitted through everything you do, and on stage all that you do is amplified. Therefore you must adjust how you feel in order to influence others to feel the same. A while ago I was the voice of Disney. I went into the sound booth and recorded the line, 'The wonderful world of Disney.' The producer said, 'Nice . . . but can you say it with a little more wonderment?'

'What do you mean?' I asked.

'Do you remember,' he said, 'when you were a little kid, coming downstairs on Christmas Day and the excitement of seeing your presents under the tree? Do you remember the first time you fell in love? Do you remember the feeling of freedom and adventure when you had your first ever car? Do you remember times like that?'

'Yes,' I said, 'I do! And I remember when I was about six years old going with my dad and seeing a Boeing 747 take off. I remember the awe and astonishment at seeing 400 tonnes of metal roaring down the runway, and taking off with the sunlight glinting on its wings.'

'That's wonderment,' he said.

The vivid memory made me have that feeling all over again, and I went back into the booth and the next take was perfect. My internal state was transmitted perfectly through just five words.

# Timing

Every conversation has a natural rhythm. I speak, then you speak. I speak, then you speak. Sometimes I pause, and you know I have more to say. Then I stop and you know it is your turn. We learn these tonal cues and rhythms and use them without any conscious effort every day.

Some people don't use them or ignore them, and as a result they are difficult to talk to. We all know people who just won't shut up and we all learn to avoid them. If those people are wise, they learn to listen more. If they are foolish they try to talk even more and even faster when they do corner us, and we learn to make greater efforts to ignore them.

Talking to an audience also has a rhythm, even if the audience is not speaking back to you. We all need a few microseconds to grasp an idea, to visualize a scene, to relish a feeling or to absorb an emotional impact. When you talk to one person you automatically sense the time they need to do this, but with an audience you can't monitor every single person. Instead you create a rhythm and a narrative with your speaking. The more you move your audience, the more time you need to give them to process what they are hearing and feeling. As you build up your rapport, you can use the pauses to amplify the impact of your words. You pause to let people absorb what you have just said, and then you can pause a little longer to build the tension about what you will say next.

Actors call this pausing 'taking a beat'. The best way to

learn this is to listen to speeches or talks by people whom you find fascinating and enthralling. Notice when and how they pause, and how they allow their audience to digest what is being said. Start by imitating them, and gradually you will evolve your own style.

## Content

What do you want to say? If I have something to say I focus on the essence of the message with the 'newspaper headline' question. Then I ask myself, 'Who is my audience?' If I am going to a small meeting there will be space to talk and time to get to know each other. I can build rapport and understand what each person needs to hear.

If I am going to a large meeting or I have to give a presentation, I have to do things differently.

The people in a large group or a crowd behave differently from how they would on their own. Each individual picks up the feelings of the people around them and also transmits them. The result is that emotions people have in common become rapidly amplified and individual differences, while still present, become less salient. In order to capture and hold the attention of a crowd, I must elicit an emotional response and then take them on a satisfying emotional journey. I have to tell a story which keeps moving so that as one emotional response finishes another is building up.

If you listen to the speeches of famous orators you will find they don't go into complex explanations because rational thinking does not unify people in the way that emotions do. There is no place for complicated reasoning in a presentation to a crowd or a large audience.

When I am crafting my message I ask myself, 'What do I want my audience to have experienced, to know and to feel when they leave the auditorium?' That focuses my message.

Finally, just before I go onstage I peek through the curtains or look at my audience and ask myself, 'What does this particular audience need?' The answer to that question tells me where to start and how to build rapport.

## Edit

I don't use written scripts or speeches. If I have a lot to remember I might write down a few bullets, but that is all. When I am preparing a speech of any sort I try to remember the golden rule of editing: 'If in doubt, cut it out.' That is true of presentations, books, TV programmes and performances of every kind from acrobatics to Zumba. Unfortunately, far too many writers, performers and producers don't stick to the rule. Funnily enough, it is often the phrase or metaphor that you are most attached to that has to go.

If you have something to say, say it as simply as possible. I have two highly intelligent friends who are each charismatic in their own way. Andrew Neill is a brilliant editor and interviewer and Sir Ken Robinson is an academic with the most-viewed TED talks in history. Although they are both extremely knowledgeable and intelligent, neither of them uses jargon, complicated explanations or long words. They listen more than they speak and they never talk down to people. They are models of eloquence because they explain themselves simply and clearly in a way that everyone can understand.

When you have made your point and delivered the right level of emotional intensity, you finish. It is far, far better to leave your audience wishing you had stayed longer than leave thinking that you were there ten minutes too long. As the old showbiz saying puts it, 'Always leave them wanting more.' One of the most charismatic people I've ever met is music producer David Geffen. He put it this way: 'Know when to leave the party.'

## IMPROVING PERFORMANCE SKILLS

*If you need to appear on stage or television or do presentations to large audiences, improve your performance skills by practising on video.*

1. Choose a simple message that takes a minute or two to speak.

2. Video yourself doing it from across the room so you see your whole body.

3. Video yourself close up – just head and shoulders.

4. Check the key performance variables:

   Presentation / styling

   Script

   Volume – appropriate for close-up and appropriate

      at a distance

   Inflections

   Timing

5. Adjust and practise elements one at a time, then re-shoot.

6. Work for 30–60 minutes a day until you are happy with your performance on film.

## Now for the magic

You have already learned a lot. What you are about to learn could change your destiny. This may be the gateway to attracting your perfect mate, to getting a promotion or making a breakthrough performance. It is your choice how to use your charisma.

I have been fascinated by charisma for years, but I did not expect to be able to teach it. I actually came across the process of releasing it completely by accident. In my years of working with people on weight-loss issues, over time I developed a series of techniques to help them change their body image. Many of them were body dysmorphics, people who have a distorted and distressing view of their own bodies. Body dysmorphia is common in people with weight issues, with anorexia and bulimia, and also occurs in some people who have suffered psychological abuse in their childhood. Some sufferers cannot even look in the mirror because they see something as hideous as a monster. Body dysmorphia is widely considered an incurable condition although I have no problem curing it.

By the way, if you suspect you have body dysmorphia and if you cannot look at yourself in the mirror, you absolutely can be helped but this technique is not for you. Seek professional help, preferably not from a conventional psychologist or psychiatrist but from someone who specializes in effective treatment, most likely from a practitioner of Neurolinguistic Programming.

I put together a four-stage process to help body

dysmorphics transform their self-image. I brought together exercises I had originally used with ordinary weight-loss clients and elements from self-esteem boosters with my latest psycho-sensory work. I tested it and after a period of trial and error I found a sequence that was powerful and reliable.

I noticed that as well as improving self-image it also seemed to increase people's confidence and vitality. So when a couple of celebrity friends came to see me feeling burnt out, I ran the same sequence with them. The effect was astonishing. They arrived feeling flat and tired and twenty minutes later they were bubbling with energy and charisma.

As I perfected and tightened up the sequence, the effect just got stronger and stronger. These first subjects were all showbiz friends, so it was not surprising that when their energy and image were boosted they were more charismatic. The next surprise, however, was that people who had no interest in or connection with show business also became more charismatic. I had stumbled upon something that didn't only change people on the inside; it changed them so much that it transformed their impact on others.

I had discovered the charisma booster.

## Four stages

The charisma booster has four parts. The first part revisits the internal dialogue which we looked at in Chapter 2. As you have already practised that you will find it easy. Now we are making specific changes in how it affects your self-image.

The second part is an adjustment of your self-image which allows you to feel peaceful and at ease with yourself, even if that is something you haven't experienced for a long time.

The third part uses a 'step-in', which is a technique by which we can borrow from the internal states of other people. I have been amazed at how powerful this technique can be when done with power and precision. I have found that as we include more and more detail of the precise physiology of our role models we access astonishingly powerful and accurate experiences of their internal states.

During the preparation for writing *I Can Make You Rich*, I worked with my colleague Michael Neill and used this technique to 'step in' to Richard Branson, Philip Green and Anita Roddick. At that point I had not met any of them, but I wanted to explore how they saw their worlds of business in order to understand their success. Michael asked me questions when I had stepped into each of them and I replied as I was guided by their physiology and perspective. I later met all three people and asked them the questions that Michael had asked me. I was amazed to hear them reply with almost exactly the same answers that I had given.

I have some theories but I still am not entirely sure how this works. All I do know is that it is astonishingly powerful. I had yet another experience of its power with Michael when I decided to step into different charismatic people during the preliminary research for this book. I chose one person, stepped into them, took on their physiology, posture and internal state, and then walked round the corner towards Michael and he took a photo of me. I went back and did the same twice more with two more charismatic people. We both then looked at the photos and I looked utterly different in each one.

I hadn't told Michael whom I had stepped into but he said, 'I think I can guess who you chose.'

'Go on,' I said.

He pointed to the photos. 'This is Billy Graham. This is Bill Clinton. This is Sean Connery.'

Michael was 100 per cent correct. That was when I knew I was on to something very, very powerful.

The fourth part is a synthesis of the most powerful, positive charismatic states.

Far more important than my description is the experience of this exercise so I want you to do it now with me. I will personally take you through all four stages of the charisma booster on the video download. As soon as you can I would like you to take twenty minutes and find a private space to watch the video download and follow my instructions.

After you have used the video download you can use the notes below as an aide memoire to repeat the charisma booster as often as you wish. However, you must use the video download for at least the first three times so that you see exactly how it should be done.

# THE CHARISMA BOOSTER

Here we bring together elements from all of this system and take them one step further. When I am physically present with people, a single run of this booster is sufficient to change their lives for ever. When I do it via a video link or recording like this download, it can take three repetitions for the full effect to kick in. However, I want to make sure you get 100 per cent of the benefits of this so I want you to do this every day for seven days.

Occasionally people tell me they feel silly standing in front of a mirror and talking to themselves. Other people say they are not sure they can find the time. My reply is always the same. It is worth feeling 'a bit silly' for a few minutes for one week when it changes your whole life for the better. If you would be willing to feel 'a bit silly' to win a million pounds you should be more than willing to feel 'a bit silly' to transform your life for the better. If someone 'can't find the time' I ask what else could be so important that you cannot find ten minutes a day for one week to improve your life for ever.

However busy you are, however silly you feel, find the time to use this charisma booster and prove to yourself this is one of the best ways you have ever spent your time.

## CHARISMA BOOSTER PART ONE

1. Stand in front of a mirror.

2. Notice which parts of your body you look at and what you say about yourself.

3. Hear what your voice says and notice where it is.

4. Look away and change your internal voice so that it sounds like Mickey Mouse.

5. Now look back in the mirror and say the same things about yourself in the voice of Mickey Mouse.

6. Do this again and again until you cannot take the voice seriously.

For example you might have said, 'I don't like my face. My belly is too big. My nose is too long. My hair is going grey.' Now you will say each of these statements with a ridiculous Mickey Mouse voice.

## CHARISMA BOOSTER PART TWO

*This critical voice has been trying to help you by offering comments and advice but it has been too harsh. If you want a child to behave better you wouldn't shout and scream, you would be encouraging. In the same way, you are learning to be nicer to yourself. You may want to change something about yourself, but first of all you need to accept yourself exactly as you are. You may want to lose weight or dye your hair or even have a nose job, but you will be in the best possible position to do that only when you accept where you are right now.*

*So now use the mirror again.*

1. Stand in front of the mirror and look at yourself.
2. Speak with your internal dialogue with your most kind and authoritative tone of voice.
3. Now speaking out loud with that kind and authoritative tone of voice, accept all the parts of yourself that you had criticized – e.g.

    'I accept my face.'

    'I accept my belly.'

    'I accept my nose.'

    'I accept my hair.'

4. Finally say with that same kind, authoritative voice:

    'I accept myself.'

    'I accept myself.'

    'I accept myself.'

5.  Keep repeating 'I accept myself' until you feel the inner sense of willing acceptance.

Remember you may well choose to change in the future but right now you are accepting where you are. When you have that feeling move away from the mirror and keep focused on the feeling. This process neutralizes all self-loathing and makes you free to change. You will practice this whole sequence every day and each time focus more and more on the feeling of acceptance.

## CHARISMA BOOSTER PART THREE

*The nervous system cannot tell the difference between a real and an imaginary situation so we are going to borrow from the self-appreciation and charisma of someone else. I would like you to think of a person who is charismatic and confident, so that when they look in the mirror they see attractiveness, beauty and sexiness. They can see when they need a haircut or whether a different tie would go better with their suit, or different shoes with their dress, but overall they are loving. That person is capable of a positive but honest critique.*

*You can choose someone you know or choose a celebrity. It does not matter whether you know exactly what they think; what matters is that you can visualize them being charismatic and confident.*

1. Stand in front of the mirror at least two paces away.

2. Close your eyes.

3. Imagine your role model standing in front of you also facing the mirror.

4. With your eyes still closed take a physical pace forward, step into them and copy their physiology. Stand the way they stand, breathe like them, become them, like a method actor.

5. Notice whereabouts in their body the feeling of confidence and charisma is strongest: for some it is in the head, for others the chest, or solar plexus.

6. When you have found the part where it is clearest or strongest, imagine the feeling has a colour and visualize that

colour where the feeling is.

7.  Make the colour richer and more intense and let it expand and then spread it all around your body to the top of your head and the tip of your toes.

8.  Now, still in the body of your role model, and feeling that colour throughout your body, open your eyes, DO NOT LOOK AT YOUR BODY YET. LOOK IMMEDIATELY AND DIRECTLY INTO YOUR OWN EYES AND HOLD YOUR GAZE FOR TWO MINUTES.

Two minutes may feel like a long time but scientific research has demonstrated that this is the minimum time required to create a massive emotional change. This look resets your perceptual filters.

## CHARISMA BOOSTER PART FOUR

*By this point you have negated the automatic critical mechanism and moved through a place of neutrality to a state in which whenever you look in a mirror it automatically generates feelings of attractiveness. But we have not finished yet. We are now going to compress the core elements to magnify the feeling and the effect.*

1. Stand in front of your mirror at least two paces away.

2. Close your eyes.

3. Remember a time when someone paid you a compliment, you knew they were sincere and it made you feel great. (If you do not have a clear memory of that, hear the compliment you would most like to hear in the world, and think of the best time and place to hear it.)

4. Return to that time and hear what you heard, see what you saw, feel what you felt as though you are there now. Play that scene over and over again and let that feeling of accepting and believing the compliment build up within you.

5. Notice where the feeling is strongest and give it a colour.

6. Make the colour richer and more intense and spread it all around your body

7. When the feeling is at its peak, imagine your role model in front of you and step into them. Take on their posture and physiology and feel their confidence and charisma fusing together with your compliment and appreciation.

8. As the two feelings blend together, open your eyes and look directly into your own eyes for two minutes.

## Lock it in place

The charisma booster is enhanced by the hypnotic trance on the audio download but you need to practise it consciously as well. Do all four parts every day for seven days to lock the effect in place. Set aside ten minutes a day, but as the effect increases you will find you don't need so much time as you move through it quicker and quicker. You will find it more and more difficult to recall the negative voice element and then even the Mickey Mouse criticism, so you will move more and more quickly to acceptance and then the step-ins.

By the end of the week it will streamline so that you do the step-ins directly to a massive boost in charisma.

## Archetypes

The charisma booster will fill you with energy and confidence and make your charisma magnetic. You can be authentic, confident and powerful. Your performance skills are brilliant. What is the final, mysterious extra something that makes it sublime?

Charisma is founded in authenticity, but it is more than that. It incorporates skills of presentation and performance, but it is more than that. Charisma connects us all because it touches what is most human in us, and yet somehow it is more than that too. Charisma is archetypal.

To understand archetypes we will have to take a step back from the practical side and look into history. All over the world humans have a great deal in common. Psychologist Paul Ekman found that there are a set of universal emotions which are recognized by all people, regardless of their specific culture. Equally, all people face the same basic challenges of life: birth, survival, education, finding food and shelter, mating, living together and facing death. And every human society tells stories.

## Star Wars

Carl Jung, the founder of Jungian psychoanalysis, recognized that the themes and characters of his patients' dreams often reflected the themes and characters of the great myths of humanity. Jung proposed that we all inherit and share a vast reservoir of myths. He named the themes and characters in those myths 'archetypes'.

Archetypal characters are ones we all recognize. In fairy tales they are characters like the princess, the king, the faithful companion and the hero. There are archetypal themes as well, like creation myths, the flood that destroys civilization and the hero's quest. Old-fashioned words and language can make it seem as if these archetypes are only relevant to history and folklore, but in fact they are still all around us, only with different names. In modern stories they are characters like the astronaut, the conman, the single mum and the rebel. George Lucas told me he drew on the work of a Jungian scholar, Joseph Campbell, to write *Star Wars*. All Lucas's characters have predecessors in the great historical myths, and the fight between The Force and The Dark Side, between good and evil, is one of greatest archetypal themes.

On the one hand, archetypes are bigger than humans. They are patterns of existence or behaviour. We can trace the archetypes in the history and myths of civilizations back to the very earliest records we have. We can see the same patterns occurring and recurring all around the world. They have existed for centuries.

On the other hand, archetypes are smaller than humans because they are only one role or character among the many different patterns and roles that humans can play. A woman may feel like a princess when she is a teenager, but she can grow up and become a mother. Every wise old man or woman was once a baby. Humans, like stories, have a beginning, a middle and an end. Archetypes are not fixed formulas but each one repeats itself, in slightly different guises, over and over again, as long as there are people alive.

## Intersection

I realized that charismatic people are extremely human and yet they have something 'more' about them. I believe that people who are genuinely charismatic are embodying an archetype.

We relate to charismatic people because they are vibrantly honest, open and human. At the same time they have an extra energy and presence. That extra energy and presence comes from the archetypes. It is as though they are resonating with, and amplified by, a pattern that is bigger than a single individual.

Charisma is the intersection of the eternal, mythical, archetypal and a single, human individual. The charismatic person has tuned into a pattern of frequency that exists at a subconscious level in all of us. That is why we all recognize charisma. And when we see charisma we are seeing two different phenomena in the same place simultaneously, which is why it is gripping and mysterious. We are seeing an eternal, immortal pattern and a living mortal person.

## The extra something

None of us control the archetypes. They were here before us and they will be here long after us. We can learn to 'tune in' to them but we can't capture them, or tie them down. Think of them like the wind. If you have a sailing boat, you can hoist your sail and catch its power, but you can't put it in a bottle and save it for later.

That extra something of charisma is like that. There is not an exercise to make it happen, it is something you will discover and feel as you step into your own charisma and then find that charisma is guiding you.

You reach deep inside for it, so that you are congruent, ruthlessly honest with yourself and nothing is blocking your energy. Then you reach out for it, let yourself feel the natural power and rhythms of the archetypal patterns you are expressing and let yourself be moved by the feelings and energy you receive. This quintessence of charisma is a gift from our ancestors and the patterns of human life that are handed down to us over generations.

## Experience

You don't need to be intellectual to be charismatic and you don't have to know anything at all about archetypes to be charismatic. Many people are naturally charismatic without knowing any of the information or exercises I have written in this book. However, I'm spelling it all out here so that every single one of us can find their way towards charisma, wherever you are starting from.

Charisma is all about other people's subjective experience and feelings. It can't be measured, photographed or proved. In the end, the reality of charisma is not in what you know, or do, or feel, but in how other people experience you. Nevertheless as you move towards it, you will increasingly feel a combination of connection and vitality, energy with a sense of ease and flow. You will experience a power that seems to come through you, because you are resonating with an archetypal pattern which amplifies your presence.

## Making it happen

You will be firmly on the path to enhanced charisma when you discover its effects are occurring even when you are not making an effort. Like riding a bicycle, when you do it, you don't have to know how to do it, or even think about it. You just decide to cycle somewhere. Your charisma will be like that.

You are free to be open to the world around you, the audience and the people you are with. If you are the focus of attention you can be completely true to yourself. You share your most personal experiences, and you will touch everyone in your audience because what is most personal is most universal.

When you feel that grace, when you feel an energy from somewhere else is guiding you, when words come easily and you sense you are magically connected to your audience, your charisma is shining. You will enter a state of 'flow' and it will seem effortless. You are in harmony with yourself, your audience and an archetypal energy that is larger than all of you. Enjoy it.

# IN A NUTSHELL

- Your charisma is grounded in your authenticity and performance and tuning into archetypal patterns

- Your charisma will be greater and your control greater the more often you use it

# NEXT STEPS

➤ Practise your performance skill as much as necessary

➤ Use the charisma booster every day for one week –
then as often as you wish thereafter

# CONGRATULATIONS!

I know that if you have read all the way through this book, practised the exercises, listened to the trance and worked with me on the video techniques, you have grasped the power to influence with both hands and you are now a more naturally charismatic person.

However, don't stop! However good you feel now, no matter how many improvements you have noticed, there is more to come!

Use the charisma booster every day for one week until it becomes second nature to automatically exude amazing amounts of charisma.

Repeat all the exercises that build your inner strength and practise all the techniques of influence until you find that one by one they become an automatic part of your communication.

Obviously, don't do anything that you don't really want to do. But if you find a particular exercise difficult, try twice as hard. If you find any exercise strange or embarrassing, do it three times as often until you actually enjoy it.

Very importantly, listen to the trance every day for a week and then use it again as often as you wish. Whenever you need a boost or you need to refresh your memory, revisit the video techniques and go through every step again. As you integrate all the elements of this system you will also find that you personally generate new variations and new styles of influence. You will express your charisma in your own unique way.

There is one last thing I'd like to give you. We can all be quick to judge ourselves these days and compare ourselves to the airbrushed images of models in magazines. I've met the most famous models in the world and I can tell you that in real life, without the make-up, the stylists and the talented photographers, they don't look like that. I'd like you to see something much more realistic: a deeper perception of beauty. On the video download you will find one more exercise called The Eyes of Love. This exercise reveals to you how you appear in the eyes of someone who loves and respects you. You will see your most wonderful and loveable qualities through a perspective that is normally hidden from you. Please take the time to enjoy it and use it as often as you like.

As you use your new-found influence and charisma, you will spread optimism and positive values throughout your life, and I believe that between us we really can make the world a better place.

I have the utmost respect for you, for wanting to better yourself.

Until we meet,

**Paul McKenna**
London 2015